FABLED SERVICE

Ordinary Acts, Extraordinary Outcomes

Betsy Sanders

The Jossey-Bass Business & Management Series

Jossey-Bass Publishers • San Francisco

FIRST PAPERBACK EDITION PUBLISHED IN 1997.
THIS BOOK WAS ORIGINALLY PUBLISHED BY PFEIFFER & COMPANY.

Jossey-Bass books and products are available through most bookstores. To contact Jossey-Bass directly, call (888) 378-2537, fax to (800) 605-2665, or visit our website at www.josseybass.com.

Substantial discounts on bulk quantities of Jossey-Bass books are available to corporations, professional associations, and other organizations. For details and discount information, contact the special sales department at Jossey-Bass.

Cover Design: Paul Bond
Interior Design, Page Composition, Illustrations: Lee Ann Hubbard

Manufactured in the United States of America.

Library of Congress Cataloging-in-Publication Data

Sanders, Elizabeth A.
  Fabled service: ordinary acts, extraordinary outcomes /
Elizabeth A. Sanders.
    p.   cm.
  Includes index.
  ISBN: 0-89384-270-2 (hardcover)
  ISBN: 0-7879-0938-6 (paperback)

    1. Customer service—Management.   2. Employee motivation.
  HF5415.5.S26   1995
  658.8' 12—dc20   94-24361

FIRST EDITION
HB Printing   10 9 8 7 6 5
PB Printing   10 9 8 7 6 5

Contents

Editor's Preface

To maintain their readership, newspapers and magazines have had to repeatedly reinvent themselves—first to combat television's sound and light, later to do battle against sound bites, and now to meet the challenge of on-line delivery and Internet information exchange.

Blessedly, books have managed to stay above the fray. Until now. The sheer mass of information available in multiple media demands that publishers take a serious look at the needs of their readers and assess how to be of service. The market is flooded with management books and portable guides to core business school curricula. Although these works offer valuable information, the problem is finding the time to wade through these erudite and often lengthy offerings.

The *Warren Bennis Executive Briefing Series* is unique. Marshall McLuhan's insight from three decades ago, "the medium is the message," possesses even more validity in today's harried world. To enhance ease and speed of content assimilation, the series makes ample use of pull quotes, bulleted lists of key points, highlighted facts, and crisp graphics. Each book presents information from renowned business leaders in the most cogent fashion, while keeping length to a minimum. Our service to you is to enable you to read and master the book's topic in one sitting. Thus, it is fitting that the first book in our series is about service.

Fabled Service is not about making customers feel good. Neither is it a one-size-fits-all prescription for customer service. More and more of your transactions are impersonal, between you and a machine. You deal with voice mail, E-mail, ATMs, and other state-of-the-art interfaces. So who cares about customer service anymore? You do.

Who warrants your business? Who do you recommend to family and friends? Whenever you talk about great service received, the subtext is individual worth. In other words, the organization delivered great service because it recognized your significance and dignity. The simple act of recognizing the primacy of the customer is a key to fabled service. Fabled service is about making an honest commitment to meeting customers' *real* needs and to winning their business. No matter how good your organization's service, there is no staying in place. Fabled service requires constant renewal and attention. Betsy's personal anecdotes, culled from years of service with a famous retailer and encounters with service legends, entertain and elucidate the key commitments required from a leader when the goal is fabled service.

Warren Bennis
Santa Monica, CA, 1995

Author's Preface

What would drive an otherwise sane person to write a book about customer service? Certainly no subject has received more attention or consumed more print in the past ten years or so. Yet, reflect on the quality of service you tolerate as a customer, client, patient, buyer, user, lessee, passenger...wherever you find yourself as a patron. Reflect on what it is like to be a customer in your own organization. Reflect on the frustration you feel as you find yourself unable to drive to realization your vision of delighting your customers because you cannot seem to infect others with that vision.

However, it can be so much better. It was my great good fortune to participate for a large part of my life in leading within an organization that is rightly fabled for its service. I came by that opportunity fortuitously, as I was unable to land a teaching job in Seattle in 1971. Economic conditions were so dire that a billboard adjacent to a major freeway exiting the city plaintively requested: "Will the last person to leave Seattle please turn out the lights?"

Desperate for work, I ignored all of my education and goals to date to gratefully accept a temporary job at Nordstrom, clerking for $2.46 an hour. That stop-gap job turned into an almost two decade career that allowed me to work with ever-larger groups of people taking care of growing numbers of customers. In 1990, when I retired as the leader of the Southern California division, Nordstrom and I had reached a milestone together: Some eleven thousand "Nordies" were delighting customers in that region at the level of one billion dollars in annual sales.

That story is an exciting one, but this book is not about Nordstrom or about retailing in general. It is about why this company and others like it have so passionately focused all of their resources on their customers. It is about how they have engaged ordinary people, people like me, in making their dreams for their business a reality. It is about what degree of dedication to their satisfaction is required for customers to make your company fabled for service.

In short, this book is about leadership. In my time with Nordstrom and in the multitude of experiences I have since enjoyed with companies from the largest conglomerate to the smallest start-up, I am convinced of one thing: Fabled service is always the product of impassioned leadership. The leadership of fabled service summons forth all our talents and energies, as well as our focused intent to excel. At the same time, it brings about a transformation, both in us personally and in the people we lead. It is at once profoundly demanding and profoundly rewarding.

Examining the real-life practice of service leadership does not provide a template for you to apply to your actions or to overlay on your organization. The specifics of what you do to maximize your opportunities for authentic service eminence are unique to you, to the rich resources at your disposal, and to the challenges you face. There is no template, but there are some very definite footsteps you can follow to widen your own path to the customer. In taking a detailed look at the fundamentals of service leadership, I hope to convey to you a sense of your tremendous potential to make a material difference, a difference so distinct that your leadership will extend far beyond your own company or organization.

I wrote this book to share with you an ideal, as well as some very practical considerations in reaching that ideal. In turn, I look forward to learning from you through your customers' enthusiastic retelling of the fables your service leadership engenders.

Foreword

Although our business was growing at a healthy rate in the seventies, the third generation of Nordstroms to run the business was concerned. We worried that we might have become enamored of our own success and, as a result, have lost some of the company's fabled devotion to serving customers. At an annual all-company management meeting, we agreed that we would focus on our concern that we had become soft on service. We would emphasize one goal—to dramatically improve customer service at Nordstrom in the coming year and to do whatever was necessary to achieve that goal.

In attendance was the most junior manager in the entire company. She had been appointed to her position just days before. She ran the newest department in a corner of our oldest, smallest store with no staff and a couple of old fixtures. Her job was to build the department by selling the merchandise herself and by enlisting the help of salespeople from adjacent departments. In the four months she had been with us as a salesperson, she had already caught the excitement of delighting customers. Now we were telling her that success as a manager meant going all out doing what she already enjoyed.

This neophyte manager, who had originally come to Nordstrom for two years to put her husband through school, was Betsy Sanders. She stayed with us for nineteen years and took our call to service as seriously as anyone we have ever known. We recognized her leadership gifts early on and kept offering her greater challenges. She met each one, always exceeding our expectations by growing in her ability to take care of the customer. In that first management job, she hit on the key to leading service: to serve the people who worked directly with the customers. She never forgot this as she went from managing our smallest department to building our largest region.

When praised for her accomplishments, Betsy claims that she simply has dedicated her life to imparting the message she took away from that meeting so long ago: Do whatever it takes to delight and serve the customer. We are pleased that she believes this. She has exemplified in her own life what we like to think of as Nordstrom service. Even more significantly, she led thousands of our employees to do the same. At Nordstrom, Betsy dedicated herself to bringing out in others their gifts to lead service in ways and to levels they have perhaps never envisioned. Now, she shares this dedication with you. We know of no other person better equipped than Betsy Sanders to inspire you and to lead you to make that commitment to fabled service.

Jack McMillan, Bruce Nordstrom, Jim Nordstrom, John Nordstrom

LEADING THE WAY TO SUCCESS AND SATISFACTION

Introduction

TO SERVE AND TO BE KIND

The congregation sat hushed, unusually attentive even for a church in which they were accustomed to hearing powerful preaching. There had been speculation all week due to the sign in front of the imposing structure that proclaimed a sermon on the unlikely theme of "The Gospel According to Nordstrom." Although members of this prosperous flock were no strangers to the Nordstrom in their neighborhood, they couldn't imagine what this mecca of merchandising had to do with Gospel principles.

The homilist, Reverend Carolyn Crawford, skillfully evoked the luxurious and bustling atmosphere of a Nordstrom store during the holidays. She recounted the sights of abundant decorations; the

sounds of holiday music expertly performed by an elegant, tuxedoed piano player; the aromas of potpourri and expensive perfume; the crowds of shoppers laden with parcels. This shared reverie was jarred, however, when Reverend Crawford introduced an improbable character to the scene: a bag lady clad in torn, filthy clothes. Convinced that this visitor's presence would be as unwelcome as it was incongruous, Reverend Crawford followed the bag lady through the store with the intent of intervening with security and softening the blow to the woman's dignity when she was asked to leave. The Reverend's original interest in this visitor, who presented such a stark contrast to the gracious abundance of the store, changed to incredulity. No one attempted to stop the bag lady as she entered the elegant and pricey Special Occasions Department. Instead, she was greeted warmly by a smartly attired saleswoman.

Reverend Crawford, eavesdropping from the adjoining fitting room, was astonished at the salesperson's solicitous responses to the customer. When the customer asked to try on evening dresses, the salesperson brought in gown after gown for the customer's discriminating inspection. With infinite patience, the salesperson carefully evaluated which were the most flattering and appropriate. When the bag lady left the fitting room, her head was held high and there was a light in her eye. She had been treated like a valuable human being.

This is what we are here for: to serve and to be kind.

When questioned about her actions by Reverend Crawford, the Nordstrom saleswoman replied, "This is what we are here for: to serve and to be kind." Reverend Crawford was moved by this act of dignity exhibited in, of all places, a department store. In addressing her congregation, she asked, "Could we say the same thing about ourselves as churchgoers? That we're here to serve and to be kind?"

The sermon's message spread far beyond the walls of the church that Sunday morning. The congregation carried the story to friends and associates. *The New York Times* highlighted the incident and that it had been memorialized in a church reputed for the quality of its preaching. Demand for the sermon was so great that the church eventually sold audiotape copies. Employees in Southern California Nordstrom stores were both humbled and challenged as they listened to the tape. Everyone agreed that the incident represented Nordstrom at its best. This story related in the sermon raised not only customer expectations but also store personnel's self-expectations. In a culture that asked employees to give their best to customers under all circumstances, the definition of best had just been raised.

THE LEGEND GROWS

The sermon represents just one more contribution, albeit a particularly powerful one, to the Nordstrom legend. Nordstrom employees are used to hearing passionate testimonials about the store and its service. Stories abound about customers who call directory assistance for a Nordstrom phone number and who are regaled with enthusiastic tales of the store's service heroics by a telephone operator.

How—in a world of big, seemingly dispassionate businesses and harried, disloyal customers and clients—does any company achieve this level of reputation? What are customers experiencing that makes a place like Nordstrom stand out in their minds? What makes the Nordstrom difference—or the Disney, Herman Miller, or ServiceMASTER difference?

The number of companies that have come to epitomize exemplary service to their customers, and thus to the world at large, is growing but still minuscule relative to the opportunity that exists. Why don't more companies share this reputation for service excellence? Why isn't your company the stuff of casual conversation or carefully crafted sermons?

Nordstrom is a company that has become fabled in the eyes of its customers. What that means, very simply, is that Nordstrom employees provide a level of service that their customers talk about. Because so many customers talk about Nordstrom's service, it has become a benchmark of service

Reportedly, one delighted customer went so far as to stipulate in her will that her ashes be scattered at Nordstrom. That way, she said, "I am certain my children will visit me often."

The level of service customers experience at Nordstrom becomes what they expect to find in other stores.... a benchmark for service everywhere....organizations start talking about "Nordstromizing" themselves...

in the retail industry. The level of service customers experience at Nordstrom becomes what they expect to find in other stores. As customers share their stories, their expectations of finding such service grows beyond retail stores and becomes a benchmark for service everywhere. From Silicon Valley start-ups to the Los Angeles Police Department, organizations start talking about "Nordstromizing" themselves, thus becoming the Nordstrom of their industry. Eventually, Nordstrom is synonymous with service.

CAN YOU AFFORD FABLED SERVICE?

Let's return to Reverend Crawford's homily so I can elaborate on two essential points that did not escape her notice. The saleswoman treated every customer like someone special because, to her, everyone was. The company obviously gave her free rein in how she worked with each customer.

The salesperson spent a lengthy time with her unusual customer. Yet, at no time did anyone sporting a manager's badge interrupt to remind the salesperson that there was more important, i.e., lucrative, work to be done. How can any company, especially yours, afford to waste time on an obviously unpromising customer? *Unpromising?* A waste of time? This one incident has achieved more productive mileage over a longer period of time than almost any I could recount. "Ah yes," you counter, "But that, of course, is something that the company could never count on."

In fact, the contrary is true. The essence of fabled service is that you can count not only on it occurring but also on it increasing in scope and in effect. To state it rather inelegantly: What goes around, comes around. And stays around. And grows. To state it as a leadership principle:

*Service is fabled when it is quite simply
the way things are done at your company.*

If you ask yourself and your people to give the very best
service to everyone at all times, that effort will bear fruit.

EVERYONE IS A CUSTOMER

I could have started with another story. Actually, the story
elements are the same, but the outcome is remarkable in
another way. It had been a hectic day and Sarah, one of our
salespeople, was quite late in taking her lunch break. As she
cut across another department to leave, she caught sight of a
woman flinging a blouse aside and stomping off.

*Not my department. Lunchtime. Angry customer. Sale
blouse. Why bother?* Sarah had none of those thoughts. Her
responsiveness to customers is so ingrained that she put
aside personal concerns and caught up with the customer
who was exiting the store. She quickly ascertained the problem. Murphy's Law had come into play: Somehow three
times the customer had asked Nordstrom to order her a
particular blouse and three times the store had let her down.
Enough was enough. This customer was fed up with Nordstrom. She preferred the nearby Neiman-Marcus anyway.
Who needed a store that couldn't care less about her?

Sarah spent the next hour trying to repair the situation.
When they parted, Sarah had not only calmed the customer
down, but also established that Nordstrom did care and
would do whatever it took to satisfy the customer's needs.

So far, the situation seems essentially the same as the
bag lady story: A very good employee spent a great deal of
time on a busy day with a very unlikely customer. Only this
time, the story has a more conventional ending. Although
there were no overt indicators, the woman Sarah helped
turned out to have shopping needs that make her the single
largest customer in Nordstrom's history. Sarah's initial mo-
tivation to attend to a customer's frustration was the same as

CATHY copyright 1994 Cathy Guisewite. Reprinted with permission of UNIVERSAL PRESS SYNDICATE. All rights reserved.

the salesperson's in the bag lady story: to serve and to be kind. The first situation resulted in tremendous good will across a broad base of people, which reflected well on the salesperson and the company. The second resulted in an extraordinary amount of business, again a win-win for the salesperson and the company.

Was it just a lucky break that Nordstrom pleased the extremely affluent customer, or finessed the situation with the bag lady while a compassionate, articulate preacher was observing and eavesdropping? No. It was not luck; it was style. Nordstrom reduces the odds of not satisfying its customers by encouraging its associates to consistently give their best in every customer interaction. They and other fabled service providers have led their organizations in such a way that the very culture encourages behavior that produces positive results on a steady basis.

*T*he key is the employees' freedom to focus on the vision: excellent customer service under all circumstances.

If the salespeople in these examples had been focused on capturing the wealthy customer or on garnering national publicity, they most likely would not have succeeded.

Greatness comes neither in doing the unusual nor in the serendipitous discovery of the extraordinary customer, but in the everyday deferential attention to each customer. It is the "everydayness" of this vision that sets it apart. *Everyone. Every day. Each customer.*

A HANDBOOK FOR LEADERS

The goal is lofty and the focus is personal: To lead your organization to such excellent service levels that you set the standard not only for your customers, but for your industry, and, indeed, for society in general.

To do less is to squander your energies, your resources, and your potential. However, as you know from experience, to achieve this level of service is neither simple nor linear.

You are the customer! This book is written with the hope that you will use it in the way it best serves your needs. It is intended to serve as a handbook for you to use in fulfilling your personal commitment to be an effective leader of a meaningful pursuit. The nature of such a commitment is perhaps best represented by a helix, which curves back around on itself but always moves up as it comes around. Thus, wherever you are in the process, the principles of service leadership provided can be applied to your situation now and will also support your ongoing development.

While the chapters are arranged consecutively, you can read them in any order. The principles do not relate to each other causally or sequentially, but at their core, which is a commitment to service.

Commitment:
To Make Service Everything Your Company Is and Does

◆ Why fabled service?
   Definitions
   Obstacles
◆ Why leadership?
◆ From principles to practice

THE ROAD
TO FABLED
SERVICE

Communicate everything you can to your associates.
The more they know, the more they care.
Once they care, there is no stopping them.

Sam Walton

1

THE ISSUE

Quality service is communicable in two ways: it can be transmitted and it can be caught. Service that is truly effective in influencing the customers' decisions is *fabled service*, that is service that becomes legendary as it is talked about by the customers themselves.

Catching whatever attitude toward service exists in the company is passive communication. It should be taken seriously because it is the best model of appropriate behavior and establishes results that are consistent with the leader's beliefs.

Furthermore, the commitment to service should be communicated through every opportunity and medium, and it should be consistent with the standard. Such communication paints the vision, sets clear goals, highlights the heroes, and celebrates the successes.

1

FABLED

Mythical

Renowned

FABULOUS!

Communication is two way, and requires not only ardent expression but also passionate dedication to listening and responding to the input of customers and employees.

WHY FABLED SERVICE?

What possible advantages could there be if your leadership provides the basis for your company's service to become fabled? What's the difference between "fabled service" and "breakthrough service," "quality service," "excellent service," or any of the other appellations that set an individual or a company apart? Let's examine the steps along the road to "fabled" service—fabulous, renowned, and mythical.

FABULOUS SERVICE

"Fabulous" conveys the sense of something that is extraordinarily positive or pleasing. Experiencing fabulous service is a wonderful event for customers. It makes them feel good, sometimes momentarily, but often on a deeper, more significant level. It can affirm for customers that they are worthwhile people. It is also a positive experience for the service provider.

The challenge to be of service or to be extraordinarily kind brings out the best in everybody.

When challenged to do whatever it takes to please the customer, employees are often amazed at how proficient they become. They learn to listen carefully for subtle clues that will help them find creative ways to delight customers.

Providing and receiving fabulous service is soul enriching, imbuing even the most mundane transaction with a sense of something done well and for a good purpose.

Fabulous service is quite simply ordinary people doing ordinary things extraordinarily well.

RENOWNED SERVICE

Have you ever driven away from a gas station chuckling over a joke the attendant just shared with you? Checked out of a hotel thinking how nice it would be to make a return visit because of the pleasant staff and surroundings? Marveled when the directions on a product were so clear that you were able to use it correctly the first time? Been touched that the shoe repair person shined your shoes after fixing them?

Pumping gas, traveling, performing household chores, and having your shoes repaired are all mundane experiences. You expect them to be run-of-the-mill, more of the same, forgettable. When instead they are delightful and linger in your mind, they give rise to another aspect of fabled service: renown. Because you have been part of an occurrence that has been lifted beyond the ordinary, you begin to tell others about it. In the telling, you are celebrating both the extraordinary attitude of the caregiver and your own importance as the object of such attention.

The company that provides exceptional service develops a reputation. You might ask:

> ### Don't all companies have reputations?
> ### Truly, no. Only the best and the worst.

Most companies have not made enough of an impression for their customers to even think about them, much less to share these thoughts with others. In order to become renowned, a company has to distinguish itself in the eyes of its customers. A company that dedicates itself to delighting the customer is in no danger of having its praises remain unsung.

> ### Customers talk if you give them
> ### something to talk about.

*B*ecause you have been part of an occurrence that has been lifted beyond the ordinary, you begin to tell others about it. In the telling, you are celebrating both the extraordinary attitude of the caregiver and your own importance in being the object of such attention.

Studies show that an upset customer tells an average of ten other people about an unhappy experience.[1]

What customers love to talk about are those truly reciprocal situations, in which the service they receive is as much a reflection on them as it is on your company.

MYTHICAL SERVICE

Once a company becomes renowned for its service, the stories begin to develop a life of their own. For example, professional speakers on customer service all seem to have one Nordstrom story in common. It seems that someone tested the company's avowed commitment to taking back all merchandise, without question, by rolling a set of tires into the store. Proof of purchase? None, for Nordstrom is a fashion specialty store and does not even sell tires. As the story goes, that did not stop the salesperson, who asked what the tires cost and then cheerfully refunded the customer's money.

*N*o advertising is as trusted as the spontaneous testimony of delighted customers.

This particular story has the Nordstrom people bemused. Asked repeatedly if it is true, they say that they have no way of knowing if such a thing really happened. However, if it did, they hope that the outcome would be just as reported. Undaunted by the lack of corroboration, believers pass the story on, and listeners get further testimonials to Nordstrom employees' dedication to service values.

When stories are told and retold, they develop the power of myth. A myth is defined as a story, ostensibly with a historical basis. In the case of your company, when myths develop, they signify that your public finds you to be extraordinary in some significant way. Stories that are told and retold make a powerful impression on customers and associates alike.

♦ Customers sharing stories affirm: This is what it means to be a customer of this company.

♦ Associates sharing stories affirm: This is what it means to work for this company.

♦ Hearing the stories, you affirm: This company reflects my values.

From the mythology, a profile develops and the company takes on a definite personality. Striving to live up to the myth fuels personal and corporate growth.

What we are calling "Fabled Service" is when the customer promotes your business. You might think of it as word-of-mouth advertising, often described as free advertising. Although no advertising is as trusted as the spontaneous testimony of delighted customers, free it decidedly is not. But it is effective. It comes at the considerable cost of inspired leadership providing dedicated associates with adequate resources to delight the customers. In other words, it costs total commitment to your customers and to your people.

FABLED SERVICE

When service is truly fabled then, it has grown to fill all of the preceding definitions. Fabled service goes way beyond the norm. Because the service is extraordinary, customers talk about it. As customers talk about service, it sets a standard for the associates of the company, including its leadership, to live up to. It also establishes a benchmark for the industry and eventually for business in general. This level of service becomes a competitive difference that is hard for others to emulate, much less to surpass. It becomes the defining level of service against which the company measures itself and against which customers measure the competition.

You have probably recognized by now the paradox inherent in the challenge to lead your organization to fabled service. The company sets the goal to provide quality service to all of its customers. Self-proclaimed service excellence is

One of the more amusing stories that took on mythical qualities over the years was about Rich's Department Store in Atlanta, Georgia. The store's dedication to customer satisfaction, particularly on returns, gave rise to a musical parody called "You Can Take Anything Back to Rich's." In this song from the seventies, the customer decided to return her pesky mother-in-law to Rich's, since she knew she could do so no questions asked.

at best disregarded by your public and at worst distrusted. It is the customer, however, who raises the level of your service reputation to a fabled status. They give their experiences with you life through frequent and public retelling.

Fabled service goes way beyond the norm. Because the service is extraordinary, customers talk about it. As customers talk about the service, it sets a standard for the associates of the company, including its leadership, to live up to. It also establishes a benchmark for the industry and eventually for business in general.

Service only becomes significant when it is so meaningful to your customers that they articulate and proclaim it.

WHY ISN'T FABLED SERVICE THE STANDARD?

Good service has been designated the sine qua non of good business for at least a decade. Yet customers, clients, patients, visitors, and guests continue to complain about increasingly indifferent service. Why has progress been so slow? Three major impediments exist:

♦ Lacking the bedrock commitment to the customer.

♦ Considering service an extrinsic aspect of business.

♦ Not understanding that someone must lead service.

COMMITTING VERSUS RESIGNING YOURSELF TO SERVICE

Across industries and organizations one simple foundation of fabled service is expressed by the attitude "We are in business to take care of the customer." A commitment to service means that you proactively set out to delight the customer, every time.

Far more common is a reactive response: Under pressure you do enough to get by or to keep even with the competition. This approach completely loses sight of reality, that the customers are the reason for your existence. Instead, you grudgingly try to figure out just how much you need to do to avoid losing business, and then do just that. Within a universe of doing everything possible to take care of your customer, you have charted a very narrow course between not being any worse than anybody else and not being any better than you have to be.

The average company loses about 20 percent of its customers annually because of poor service.[2]

MAKE SERVICE AN INTRINSIC VALUE

If one belief seems to underlie less-than-fabled service, it is that service is simply a commodity—something learned about from outside sources and applied when timing and resources permit. It is simply one more approach to doing business; one that is enjoying an annoying trendiness.

It may seem that an inordinate amount of your time and the company's resources are devoted to raising the level of service, yet the only consistent result is disappointment. Frustrations mount as you find yourself unable to surmount the same stumbling blocks:

THE FAR SIDE   By GARY LARSON

"Wait! Wait! Listen to me! . . . We don't HAVE to be just sheep!"

- ♦ An inability to communicate your vision throughout the organization frustrates you.
- ♦ Constant firefighting diverts you from focusing on service.
- ♦ Overburdened budgets do not allow you to add a service improvement project.
- ♦ Price seems to drive customers' decisions.

Companies That Raised the Bar

INDUSTRY	FIRM
Airlines	Alaska Airlines, Reno Air, SAS, Southwest Airlines
Diversified Services	Federal Express, IBM, Intuit, UPS
Entertainment/ Hospitality	Club Méditerranée, Marriott Hotels, Ritz-Carlton, Walt Disney
Financial Institutions and Services	First Chicago, Home Savings, USAA
Retailers	Calyx & Corolla, Fresh Choice Restaurants, The J. Peterman Company, L.L. Bean, Lands' End, McDonald's, Nordstrom, ServiceMASTER, Smith & Hawken, Tattered Cover Book Store, Wal★Mart

♦ Quality employees to provide the envisioned service are either unavailable or unaffordable.

♦ The focus on service must be postponed until you complete this quality initiative (or reengineering plan, or ISO 9000 program, or...).

♦ Customers do not care about this level of service.

♦ Your company is either too small or too big to distinguish itself through service.

♦ General service level is so mediocre that you can look good with no effort.

♦ Competitors' service is so superior to yours that you are focusing your resources elsewhere.

♦ Been there. Tried that. It doesn't work for you.

If you share these frustrations, you probably also share the viewpoint that service is nice to have but nonessential to the business at hand.

You can spend enormous amounts of time, energy, and resources on isolating service, on seeing it as a program or a value or a goal that your company must adopt in order to compete or to survive. As long as you seek to add an external dynamic to your business, the results will be disappointing. Service begins to be meaningful when it is an internal dynamic. This dynamic develops when you accept service as the underpinning of your enterprise, believing that without your customers, you would not exist. When the rationale for providing service becomes simply "That's what our customers deserve," you will have begun the journey of leading your company to being a fabled service provider. Nordstrom says it very simply:

A company that believes it exists to serve the customer develops its unique resources—in partnership with its employees—to take very particular care of its customers.

> **The customer is the reason for our business.**

With this principle firmly in mind, the focus on the customer becomes internal. A company that believes it exists to serve the customer develops its unique resources—in partnership with its employees—to take very particular care of its customers. This then is the foundation of all fabled service, no matter what the industry, its size, its complexity, or its geographic location.

COMMIT TO SERVICE LEADERSHIP

The essential difference between companies where service is the fundamental structure and companies without this foundation lies in leadership—or the absence thereof. It is appropriate at the beginning of this journey to examine the principle underlying the kind of leadership that will raise your company to the level of fabled service. Looking at the nuts and bolts of other people's service programs is looking at the wrong end.

> *Observed techniques are not the process of servicing the customer; they are the outcome of a process that has its origin in the commitment of the leader.*

The footprints to follow if you are to achieve fabled service are the commitments themselves.

When it comes to values, there are two levels of commitment you make: the "yes" you say and the "yes" you live. If you are to be a leader of service, you must be prepared to live out your service principles on an ever-deepening basis.

Is making a commitment to be of service in order to lead service rational or even possible? Consider Albert Schweitzer's words:

> *There is no higher religion than human service. To work for the common good is the greatest religion.*

The word religion has its roots in a Latin word, meaning to bind together. Schweitzer is saying then, that service, of all human endeavors, has the greatest power to bind our lives together, to make them whole, to give them meaning.

It is this level of commitment, when service becomes the essence of what you do and how you act, that allows you to develop service within your organization to the level that you envision.

From Philosophy to Practice

Actually, the pursuit of fabled service, so seemingly complex and elusive, is in reality quite simple and attainable. Fortunately, our lived commitments not only form an irresistible dynamic force but also leave footprints. Footprints that can be tracked. Likewise, service buffs leave footprints for us to follow. What they *say* may be very clear. What they *do* is unmistakable. Their commitment provides us with more than just a "how-to." It lays out why to commit and why to persist.

FABLED SERVICE AS YOUR JOURNEY

Tracking the footprints of those who are acknowledged service leaders is not the same thing as attempting to adopt someone else's program or persona wholesale. You may have already experienced failure at that. Instead, dedicate yourself to learning the essential practices of committed service leaders and then make a commitment to incorporate these practices in your business.

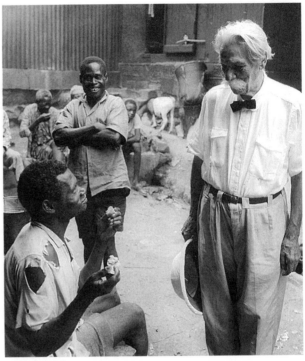

AP/Wide World Photos

Dr. Schweitzer stops to talk to a patient during a tour of his hospital near Lambarene, Gabon, Africa.

Remember, there is no ninety-day money back service guarantee. The pursuit of fabled service is a lifelong quest. It begins whenever you dedicate yourself to it and ends when you abandon it. You will never reach the ultimate destination: perfect service with every customer, in all situations, at all times. However, it is in striving to approach that destination that you grow into excellence.

Also, if your service is going to set you apart, you are going to have to think about service fundamentally differently than you have in the past. While it is true that every

---

The Power of the Right Vision[3]

Attracts commitment and energizes people

Creates meaning in workers' lives

Establishes a standard of excellence

Bridges the present and future

—**Burt Nanus**

Do not relegate your consideration of service to the quality of interaction that takes place at the point and time of sale....You have to start to think about your service as your customer does: Service is everything your company is and does.

journey consists of thousands of steps, do not think incrementally, think strategically. Ask yourself: What do I really want to create for our customers? What will it take to create what I want?

If you are going to lead your company to fabled service, you have to think of service far more broadly than what takes place at the point of sale. Start to think about your service as your customer does: Service is everything your company is and does. You have to manage every aspect of your business for service excellence. You will integrate service with everything you do. Service is not a discrete cost center; it is part of all costs of doing business. And because service is doing what is meaningful to the customers, service will always impact revenues—positively.

Finally, you need to frankly acknowledge how often your attempts to manage service are attempts to figure out what to do to get "those people out there" to behave better. Your commitment, as a leader of fabled service, is to concentrate on your own opportunities for growth. Your challenge is to serve the people who serve the customers and to promote their growth in excellence.

REFLECTIONS

♦ Fabled service is the only level of service that makes a significant difference to your customers.

♦ Fabled service means customers know why they choose and promote your business passionately.

♦ Fabled service requires commitment.

♦ Fabled service is an intrinsic value of your business.

♦ Fabled service is based on focused leadership.

♦ The leader's passion for the customer is lived out in broad, clear commitments.

♦ Lived commitments are the footprints that allow others to follow and learn how to create fabled service.

♦ The leader's vision of fabled service should engage the resources and commitments of all constituents.

ACTION STEPS

Commit to leading fabled service that is so meaningful that your customers proclaim it.

Understand that greatness comes in striving toward goals that can never be fully attained.

Envision how great service could be; what currently exists will not engage your people or your customers.

Expect results! Service that doesn't improve your business is not truly service to your customers.

Dream the dream, share the vision, support the effort, and celebrate the results.

*C*ommitment:
To Be of Service
in All That You Do

- ♦ Make a habit of service
- ♦ Learn from service legends
- ♦ Set expectations and model behavior

FABLED SERVICE
IS A WAY
OF LIFE

Excellence is an act won by training and habituation.
We do not act rightly because we have virtue or excellence,
but rather we have those because we have acted rightly.
We are what we repeatedly do.
Excellence then, is not an act, but a habit.

Aristotle

2

THE ISSUE

There is no matrix you can superimpose upon your organization to create and to nurture quality service. Service is first and foremost a mindset, an attitude, a commitment.

Fabled service cannot be confused with techniques or services implemented to meet specific customer needs or to respond to competition. Services play a role in developing a service culture, but are not significant in isolation. To be meaningful, services must stem from a genuine commitment to be of service, rather than from piling on techniques.

Service, in short, is not what you do, but who you are. It is a way of living that you need to bring to everything you do, if you are to bring it to your customer interactions.

15

LIVING THE LEGEND

My interest in Wal★Mart began in the early eighties, when visiting analysts told me how much this upstart company, founded by Sam Walton and headquartered in Bentonville, Arkansas, reminded them of Nordstrom. They were confounded not only by its growth but also by its spirited culture. While Wal★Mart focused on the low-end commodity side of the business, contrasted to Nordstrom's growing secure niche in the fashion merchandising area, the analysts noticed a marked similarity in energy and exuberance—and in customer response. Intrigued, I set out to learn what I could about this company.

As the hype about Wal★Mart increased, the media became increasingly intrigued with its founder, Sam Walton, and the tone of the remarks changed from an initial gentle derision of him as a good ol' boy to reverence for his genius. At Nordstrom, the cardinal virtue has always been humility. The cardinal vice was being "...a legend in your own mind." Thus, I was prepared to be at least mildly disappointed in Sam Walton the Man versus Sam Walton the Myth.

My first exposure to Mr. Sam, as this hero was affectionately and universally called, came at one of the most avidly reported Wal★Mart events of all, the fabled Annual Shareholders' Meeting. As a rule, CEOs abhor shareholders' meetings and try to have them in out-of-the-way places at inconvenient times. That way, perhaps few outsiders will show up to ask questions. "True to form..." I thought, as I received the invitation and noted the time of 7:00 a.m. and the University of Arkansas Field House location. It was true to form—Sam Walton's extraordinary personal form.

When I arrived a few minutes before seven, Mr. Sam was already center stage and having the time of his life. What followed was five solid hours of celebration. The chairman of Wal★Mart had something to celebrate: another year of record-breaking business. In fact, this was the year the company had become the number one retailer in America. The meeting, however, was no self-congratulatory tribute; the

After Sam Walton died, the Wal-Mart management team changed the hyphen in the company's name to a star in memory of its founder.

reason it took five hours was because there were so many people to thank.

RECOGNIZING PRIORITIES

First and foremost the focus was on the associates. The reason we were in this sports arena became clear. Every single company store selected one or two stockholder associates to represent them at this meeting in Bentonville. The representatives were responsible for getting themselves there, and

Arkansas Democrat-Gazette

Sam Walton addresses a gathering of associates.

get there they did, some four thousand of them! They carpooled and came by bus. They took trains and planes and every other conceivable mode of transportation. They were there to be honored and they were honored to be there. Their spirit could not be contained.

Mr. Sam recognized them by region, by store, by merchandise categories, by heroics, by special talents, by sales innovations. He cut that fabulous year's business every way he could to express gratitude to as many stores and teams as possible. Perhaps most touching were the number of associates who attended in military uniform. The company had invited every associate who had served in Operation Desert Storm to attend as a special guest.

As the field house filled to capacity and then well beyond, Mr. Sam became concerned that some of the associates had to stand. What did the wealthiest man in America and CEO of the world's most successful retail company do? He invited those standing to come forward and sit on the stage. A couple hundred of them bashfully responded. After their initial embarrassment, they became caught up in the spirit of the event and became the chorus for all the cheering that was coming from Sam.

The accolades continued. Vendors were thanked and the most successful partnerships were highlighted. Of particular importance were those manufacturers who had worked with Wal★Mart to keep or create jobs in the United States. Shareholders were thanked for their confidence and stock analysts for their shrewd support. Every single part of this mammoth business was examined, and the contributions of each department were extolled. Most of all, this meeting was a celebration of customers. The tribute focused on how everyone had helped Wal★Mart delight more customers than anyone else in history.

Somewhere along the way, the usual business of a shareholders' meeting was attended to, and then it was time to adjourn. Rob Walton, the oldest of Sam's offspring, came to the microphone. "Now all you associates, don't forget: You're invited to Mom's and Dad's for lunch."

I arrived at "Mom's and Dad's" before the crowd. The Waltons' home, built in 1970, is lovely but comfortable rather than ostentatious. Situated on a stream in the middle of a parklike setting, it exudes family. This is where I first met Mr. Sam face to face. He expressed delight that I could be there, as if it were his distinct honor rather than mine. After a few minutes of business chit-chat, he excused himself, expressing anticipation of us having more chance to talk over the next three days. "You see my bosses lining up over there?" he asked, motioning to a part of the garden where several hundred people were cheerfully lining up. "They all want a chance to speak with me. I don't know why it is important to them, but it is. That means it is important to me."

As we watched over the next several hours, this man greeted every single one of the four thousand or so associates who were his guests that day. Never once did he show a sign of concern for himself, but he demonstrated obvious delight in being with these special people. That he was in his seventies, or that he had already stood on the stage for five hours, or that he might be affected by the cancer that had been diagnosed ten years before, was never in evidence. Instead, he called each person by name—carefully noted from their traditional Wal★Mart nametags, shared anecdotes, signed autographs, and posed for photos. It would not be an exaggeration to say that for each Wal★Mart associate this was a major life event.

> *Sam Walton's gift of mirroring the best in the other person and then thanking that person for being terrific was in evidence throughout the rest of my visit.*

As we talked business, he sent me out on assignments. "Visit our distribution center would you, and tell me how we could improve." "What did you think of our new store concept?" "Tell me how Nordstrom gets its buyers to work on the selling floor with the customers? How would you do that here?" I realized to my utter amazement that he was picking my brain! The world's most successful retailer thought that I had something worthwhile to share. I found myself expressing ideas I had not ever articulated before, surprising myself at my own knowledge and abilities.

Everywhere we went, Mr. Sam acknowledged the people who worked and shopped at Wal★Mart. Nothing distracted him from being responsive to the associates and customers who were the heart of his business.

Some contemporaries of Sam Walton who knew him when he was doggedly working to turn a concept based in northwest Arkansas into a way of life for Americans everywhere, tend to downplay his accomplishments. "Anyone could have done what Sam Walton did!" they bluster. "He just got very lucky."

Service Legends Hall of Fame

Leon Bean	L.L. Bean	Manufacturing
Max De Pree	Herman Miller	Manufacturing
William Hewlett David Packard	Hewlett/Packard	Technology
J. Willard Marriott	Marriott Hotels	Hospitality
Stanley Marcus	Neiman-Marcus	Retailing
William McKnight	3M Corporation	Manufacturing
J.C. Penney	J.C. Penney Corporation	Retailing
Sam Walton	Wal★Mart	Retailing
Thomas Watson, Sr.	International Business Machines	Manufacturing

Mr. Sam's "good fortune" was that he loved his business. He never tired of seeking out better ways to serve his customers. As his business grew, so did his appreciation for those who made it happen. Sam knew that the customer was the very reason for the business. He lived out this belief in everything he did. And in his passionate living out of this belief, he left unmistakable footprints for everyone to follow.

SERVICE IS A WAY OF LIFE

Your commitment to be of service yourself always is the foundation of fabled service leadership. Sam Walton recognized this clearly when he repeatedly acknowledged:

Great leaders are what they want their companies to become.

Service starts with leaders living out the visions they have for their companies. Remember, fabled service consists in ordinary people doing ordinary things in extraordinary ways. Sam Walton believed this. So do the Nordstroms. So do the other service legends. This is as true for you as it is for the people you lead. Your people are going to gauge what is important to you by how you respond to your day-in and day-out responsibilities. Greatness develops neither in crisis situations nor in the big deal, but in the handling of the everyday, run-of-the-mill details of life.

Do you complain about all the "theys" who are not getting the message and, thus, send a message of disdain for your employees? Are you involved in such important matters that you have neither the time nor the inclination to be available to customers?

What Habits Do Service Legends Practice?

Possess and live out their vision

Take action

Teach and learn, throughout life

Set high expectations for themselves/others

Live what they want their company to become

Develop authentic commitments

The real crisis occurs when leaders pontificate about what they want for their companies while undermining the visions through their own practices.

THE DEVELOPMENT OF EXCELLENCE

Quite simply, your priorities show up clearly in your planner—not on the side of the page that shows what you have set goals to do, but on the side that shows hour by hour what you actually got done. Your priorities show up in your check-book, not necessarily in your budget. How you allocate personal resources has a bearing on how you allocate the company's. The allocation of resources—time, money, attention—demonstrates the breadth and depth of your commitment.

IBM

Tom Watson, Jr., and Tom Watson, Sr., founder of IBM

It can be very disconcerting to consider that our actions express the true extent of our commitments. Consider this simple thought from a consummate leader, Thomas Watson, Sr.:

> *Nothing takes less time to acquire than excellence.*

Watson maintained that the only thing someone needs to do to be excellent is to stop doing less-than-excellent things.

What relevance does this have for us as service leaders? Tom Peters had this to say:

> Suppose you commit to new heights in quality or service here and now. In your mind, you're an

Thomas J. Watson, Sr., used to promote his vision of a constantly improving organization with a sign that read simply THINK.

instant Nordstrom or Motorola. But, your next task—dratted real world!—is to go through your boring in-basket. What an opportunity! So you don't know much about Nordstrom or Motorola; nonetheless, respond to the first item in your in-basket as you imagine a Nordstrom or Motorola exec would.

A memo from a front-line worker complaining about a silly roadblock to improvement? A request to change office-supply vendors? An irate note from a customer or distributor? "Nordstrom" it. "Motorola" it! Act out, in a small way, your Nordstrom-Motorola fantasy of matchless quality.[1]

Pretending turns to practice, and continued practice moves us toward perfection. It takes an instant to stop doing the less-than-excellent thing and a lifetime of practice to maintain doing the excellent. With every flex of the excellence muscle, it becomes easier, stronger, and more ingrained.

Look again at Peters' example of attacking the in-basket. Here, the everyday task diverts attention and depletes time, just when you would like to be focused on projects that promise greater rewards. However, it is in practicing excellence in the small things that you prepare yourself to handle the major with quality.

Remember, fabled service consists in ordinary people doing ordinary things in extraordinary ways.

DEEDS, NOT WORDS

How does this apply to service? Completely. Just as with your children, your employees pay scant attention to what you say and keen attention to what you do. There is no area in which living out your vision is more sensitive than in this area of service.

After all, service is nothing more than a reflection of the esteem in which you hold others. Your employees can gauge your commitment to customers by how you treat people—including them—every day.

If customers are truly the reason you are in business, the people who take care of those customers are your most significant concern. You express your commitment to customers through your daily interaction with employees. They get their signals directly from you. Do you want to know the level of service your customers are getting? Take a candid look at how you treat your secretary, the janitor, the "rank and file."

It takes an instant to stop doing the less-than-excellent thing and a lifetime of practice to maintain doing the excellent....it is in practicing excellence in the small things that you prepare yourself to handle the major with quality.

WHAT DO YOU REALLY EXPECT?

Typically, you give a lot of thought to what you wish your people would become. You are frustrated because you have such great vision for your business and don't understand why employees can't figure out how to achieve it. The problem is that you are ignoring the awful truth, that your people reflect your actual expectations. It is a rare employee who doesn't try to please the boss. So if you don't like what is going on in your offices or on the shop floors, it is probably not that _they_ are not getting the message, it is that you are not giving your employees the message that you think you are.

THE POWER OF MODELING BEHAVIOR

Little things are everything, when it comes to signals. I learned long ago that, however thorny the problems I was grappling with in my office, when I hit the selling floor, that was where my full concentration had to be. If I walked around frowning over that lease negotiation that was going wrong or the shipment that was tied up in customs, everyone who caught sight of me was quite certain we were doomed and that she or he was the direct cause.

Likewise, if I walked by a ringing phone, rather than diving for it, so could the staff. If I did not stop to assist a customer who appeared confused, they could too. If I ignored a man waiting impatiently for his wife to come out of the fitting room and did not check to see if a cup of coffee or that day's paper wouldn't ease the boredom, why should anyone else be concerned?

The power of example in customer interactions came home vividly to me after I left Nordstrom. I was hired by a closely held retailer, whose top management knew me well, to come in and "Nordstromize" their sales force. They told me how they had always insisted that customer service was to be everyone's number one goal, but nobody seemed to pay any attention. They were ready to fire all of their store personnel and start over with a more talented bunch. Before going to that extreme, they wanted me to see if I could figure out what was wrong with their people and suggest a cure.

I began by visiting at least half of their few dozen stores. In each store, I had the same experience. The stores themselves enjoyed fair to very good locations, were attractively designed and well laid out, and generally presented a customer-friendly appearance. As soon as I walked in, I spotted the people working there, so there appeared to be adequate staff. However, the cashier was invariably bent over some sort of paperwork, deep in concentration. There would always be one or two people counting merchandise and writing their findings down on clipboards. A couple of others would be busy with dust mops and glass cleaner. Everyone else was busy toting boxes of new merchandise out of the back rooms and stacking it on the shelves.

No one looked up. No one acknowledged my presence, nor that of any of the other would-be customers who had been lured into this environment by advertising, window displays, or the beautiful merchandise that could be spied from the mall or parking lot. You have undoubtedly been there yourself only too many times.

When I interrupted any of these busy employees to ask for assistance, they were cordial enough but obviously stressed. After all, they had tasks to complete and to walk me around or to ring up my purchase would cut into their time.

I invited the executives to make store tours with me. This time we were not so invisible: Everyone knew when the boss came through the door. If their entrance hadn't been noticed, the executives made their presence known by dramatically launching into store inspections, their dissatisfaction growing with each breach of standards noted.

No, the bosses were not happy. They made a great show of running their fingers across the shelves and blowing off dust. They carried reports showing which stores were behind on paperwork, and they held discussions about less-than-expected follow-through in each store. They noticed where stock was low or new merchandise had not made it to the floor. Any excuse was met with impatience. The suggestion that the employees had been too busy with customers to get the housekeeping done made the owners absolutely irate.

Not a word was said about the customers who walked through the store without being greeted. As customer after customer left the store empty-handed, the employees were never once questioned about what the shoppers had wanted. Sales were never discussed. In fact, no notice was made of the customers or of the business itself—selling merchandise. The entire focus was on running a tight ship.

When we are observing someone else's business, the lesson is often clear. However, these otherwise smart people were dumbfounded when I suggested that there was nothing wrong with their employees. Like most sane people, their people were doing everything they could to meet their bosses' expectations. These expectations, as the executives demonstrated in every store we visited, just had nothing to do with customer service and satisfaction.

What do you really pay attention to in your people's performance? If your goal is service, but you don't model, measure, or reward service, what role model do your people have to follow?

*Your very best people will respond to
what you actually do, what you evidently
measure, and what you openly
reward—every single time.*

Monomaniac With a Mission

It was Leon Royer who coined the phrase "monomaniac with a mission" to describe those whose focus is unmistakable. When you hear that phrase, surely someone you have worked for comes to mind.

We need to become monomaniacs with the mission of providing fabled quality service to our customers. I think of Sam Walton, baseball hat cocked slightly to the side, walking through his stores and shaking the hands of astonished customers. "How have we been treating you? Are you finding what you came in for? Do you have any thoughts on how we could serve you better?"

This simple behavior had real impact on the customers as well as on all of the associates present. But Sam was never a person to waste time or energy. He wrote the customer's suggestion down in the notebook he always carried, or he recorded it on a small tape recorder. Then he would follow up, cementing forever the reality of his concern.

It is this monomaniacal focus that most sets the Nordstroms apart from other leaders that I have known. The Nordstroms simply never let up; they are ardent, vocal champions of customer service excellence. More effectively, however, they practice this concern in all that they do.

One instance in particular taught me more than any motivational speech, class, or contest ever could have. At the time, I had been with the company three years and seemed to have gotten the message. I was motivated and, in turn, had motivated the departments that I had managed. Nonetheless, when I looked up one afternoon to find five Nordstroms walking through one of my departments, I experienced a not unnatural sense of panic. Mind you, I had heard over and over that the real boss came in every day when the doors opened and stayed until closing, but who can take a visit from the five chief executive officers with equanimity? My quick review of the department revealed no obvious flaws. They seemed to be merely using my department as a throughway to the store manager's office, so I began to relax. Then Bruce Nordstrom became visibly distressed. Sighting me, he peeled off from the group.

"Betsy, how did we fail those two women?" he asked, pointing to customers heading for the exit. I had not even noticed the pair, so had no answer. "Well," he continued, "they were just saying they have never been so disappointed in their whole lives. Please go find out what happened."

Already chagrined, I raced after our departing guests, not sure how to stop their determined retreat. Failing to come up with anything couth, I blurted out that Mr. Nordstrom was concerned because he had overheard them expressing disappointment with the store. Their surprise at being accosted turned to pleasure at his thoughtfulness. They explained it was not the store that had disappointed them, but life. They coveted a dress they could not begin to afford.

The dress they loved was in our most expensive department. I managed the moderate dress department. So after encouraging them to show me the object that had upset their equilibrium, I invited them into my fitting rooms and kept them busy trying on beautiful things they could afford. This time when they headed for the exit, they each had two dresses in their possession and smiles on their faces.

This really made an impression on me. Here I was, working the floor, oblivious to potential customers. Not only had Bruce Nordstrom's concern meant selling four dresses that day, it had ensured that these customers would be back. And most certainly, they would regale their friends with the story every time they wore one of those dresses.

I was particularly struck by the fact that Bruce Nordstrom had been observing the customers, even while he was on the way to do something very important, in this case as it turned out, to negotiate the lease for a new store. This was an important lesson for me, who could find myself distracted from taking care of the customers by some of the simple stock-keeping duties of a department manager. The sincerity of his concern was cemented for me when, after five hours of tough negotiation, he came out of the meeting and said, "I know you took care of those customers. I just am curious what was wrong and what you did about it."

How many management classes would I have needed to attend before I internalized what I learned that day? The Nordstroms always said that customer service was our most important duty. Bruce Nordstrom, in a simple interchange, vividly lived out his commitment. Not only did he serve as a model for how I treated customers henceforth, he taught me how to lead.

> *The most effective leadership I could*
> *exercise was not in what I said, no matter*
> *how compellingly, but in how I acted.*

PRACTICE ON THE SMALL THINGS TO BE PERFECT ON THE LARGE

If you asked me where I left the biggest service footsteps, I would probably think of momentous occasions. Perhaps it was during the flood, or the time the transformer exploded on opening day. Or, maybe it was when we built the original team to open our first Southern California store. Then there was the two-day motivational course through which I personally led everyone in the region in groups of twenty.

However, if you asked the people I led when they learned the most from me, you probably wouldn't hear about any of these events. Granted, sometimes they mentioned a speech I gave at a store meeting, or a column I wrote in our in-house paper. Far more often, they would relate some little incident I had long forgotten. Perhaps it was that I never wanted a salesperson to pay attention to me if there was a customer anywhere in sight. Or that I handled the telephone if it was ringing in a department where everyone else was occupied. Or that I would see a customer waiting at the desk with a return and take care of it. Quite often, their responses related to quiet personal moments, when I remembered to ask about their sick child or to congratulate them on a great customer service letter. Little things. Things that had become second nature to me over the years. Things that I learned from observing the Nordstroms. Things that show a real commitment to the customers—and to the employees who served them.

BEING OF SERVICE IS A JOURNEY

If you do not understand your own development as a process, it could be daunting to consider the footprints left by the service legends. In order to avoid feeling inferior, it is easier to relegate Sam Walton to the "lucky" pile and to dismiss Bill Gates as a "genius." "The Nordstroms inherited their business, after all." And so it goes. Service legends are considered from the perspective of their success, rather than from how they got there. In reflecting on their own accomplishments, however, our heroes present a very relatable perspective.

For instance, Sam Walton, in speaking of the growth of Wal★Mart, remarked wryly, "And like most other overnight successes, it was about 20 years in the making." Bud Walton had this to say when asked to comment on how his brother achieved what he did:

> From the time we were kids, Sam could excel at anything he put his mind to. I guess that is just the way he was born. Back when he carried newspapers, they had a contest. I've forgotten what the prize was—maybe $10, who knows. He won that contest going out selling new subscriptions door-to-door. And he knew he was going to win. It's just the makeup of the man. [2]

Determination...Staying with the journey...Sticking to the path...Those are the options open to all of us. Particularly on the journey to service quality, the only itinerary that will get you there is to keep plugging away. Lasting service improvement never comes through quick fixes. Magic formulas do not exist. Service happens when you hit it again, every day, day in and day out. It is a determined mindset, a serious commitment, and an optimistic expectation. Being excellent is not something we achieve and then check off.

> *The major challenge in taking care of the customer is you never become so good at it that you can quit working on it.*

Your strategy has to be consistent and persistent, no matter what. You cannot support service efforts when the ink is black and business is good, then turn off that support when there is a downturn. Service is not a program, but a process, not a luxury, but of the essence.

REFLECTIONS

♦ Fabled service is a way of life.

♦ Everyday heroes help us believe in our potential to succeed.

♦ Fabled service happens when ordinary people do ordinary things in extraordinary ways.

♦ Your priorities become your people's priorities.

♦ To be excellent, stop doing less than excellent things.

♦ People respond to monomaniacs with missions. Share your passion!

♦ Being of service is a process that you will be perfecting the rest of your life.

ACTION STEPS

Be a conscious competent.

Become a student of service. Read and observe all that you can about those who have based their lives on empowering others.

Monitor yourself. Hear what you say. Gauge your responses to employees and customer situations. What do you need to change to practice what you preach?

Work on developing good service habits, one by one. Today, pick the first less than excellent thing that you are going to stop doing—and the first excellent thing that you are going to practice. Track your new habits as they develop.

Expect the best of the people you serve, both employees and customers. Provide an environment in which people can excel.

Reward good service in all of your dealings.

Accept the paradox: Being of service is a process that you will be perfecting the rest of your life. At the same time it is a day in and day out commitment. Be patient with yourself as the good service habits become ingrained. Do not let lapses become bad habits.

*C*ommitment:
To Act on the Belief That You Are in Business to Serve Customers

♦ Respond to customer needs—and wants

♦ Know your customer

♦ Examine every point of contact with the customer

♦ Benchmark against the best

Fabled Service Is Defined by the Customer

Perhaps the cardinal rule of customer service is:
Know thy customer!

Karl Albrecht

3

The Issue

Delivering quality service means that you do well the things that are important to the customer. Doing things well that are not important has no impact. Actually, the only time customers are impressed by service is when it goes well beyond their expectations. Not meeting their expectations is their definition of poor service.

Providing fabled service requires careful attention to the changing needs and desires of the customers, making them the drivers of your business. Fabled service begins with understanding the customers' expectations as the baseline and then seeks to consistently and relevantly improve service delivery to continually delight the customer.

33

If the Customer Does Not Care About It, It Is Not Service

When Nordstrom entered the California market in 1978, it used a "come as we are" strategy rather than attempting to outdo the reigning, sophisticated stores at their own games. In most cases, this provided a point of difference that the customers appreciated; however, in at least one area, we made an erroneous assumption about what would please customers.

Anyone familiar with Nordstrom's Seattle headquarters knows about the city's weather; it rains—a lot. Consequently, Northwestern homes tend to be warm, snug shelters from the drizzle. That is how we built our Northwestern stores and that is how we planned our beautiful California store. We created wall and floor coverings in deep tones of dark colors: shades of burgundy, navy, and hunter green were used throughout the store. As a point of quality, a real service to our customers, we used only incandescent lighting. No fluorescent tubes for us, with their harsh, color-distorting glare. Our departments were cozy caves illuminated by subdued, natural lighting fixtures. The elegant, comfortable atmosphere seemed just right to us.

The response to our decor was almost comical. Customers entered the store from the invariably sunny parking lot and groped their way through the clothing fixtures. Squinting, they held the merchandise up, twisting it this way and that under the dim lighting in an attempt to gauge color or to read sales tags. They would apologetically ask if they could walk the merchandise over to the single skylight or out into the mall so they could see it better.

Complaints about the lighting far outnumbered all other comments. At this point, we never questioned whether the come-in-out-of-the-rain atmosphere might be inappropriate for Southern California's Eden-like climate. We were absolutely convinced that incandescent or "true" lighting was the only appropriate choice in a quality store that was concerned about the customer. So we added more fixtures and we increased the wattage. We added tracks to the ceilings and cans to the tracks. We doubled the fixtures and wattage in our second store. Nevertheless, the dark walls and ceilings continued to absorb all available light and our customers continued to squint and complain.

A by-product of our insistence on providing this decor was the electric bill. Power rates were about ten times higher in Southern California than in the Northwest. As we lamped up our stores, our customers may not have been any happier, but the utility company certainly was. We were putting more and more energy, both literally and figuratively, into our lighting. What we thought should make our customers happy was having exactly the opposite effect; they were liking it less and less. And, they were getting tired of telling us the exact reason for their displeasure, only to have us respond by providing more of the same and trying to convince them they should love it.

After a couple of years of trying harder and harder to implement our concept of the proper shopping environment, we finally realized what the customer was telling us: lighten up! By the third store we got it right, creating an open, airy environment in which the light reflected cheerfully off sand, taupe, and natural colors. Plus, we replaced all those light bulbs (which also burned out with alarming rapidity) with true color-enhancing fluorescent fixtures, the very products we had disdained as not good enough for our customers in the first place. The electric bills went down, and so did the complaints.

THE CUSTOMER KNOWS BEST

In retrospect, it is obvious that Nordstrom was not following its own credo when it insisted on creating a shopping environment both out of touch with the market and quite expensive to boot.

> *Much time, money, thought, and effort went into providing enhancements for the customers that were actually barriers to their satisfaction.*

How many times do you make similar errors in your own business?

Often, very successful companies are the most vulnerable to assuming that they know exactly what the customers want. Over the years, I became accustomed to hearing associates dismiss customers' requests with the observation that the desired item "just isn't Nordstrom." This meant that whatever the customer requested did not fit Nordstrom's concept of what was appropriate for our customers. In this way we resisted selling such items as short-sleeved dress shirts for men in the summer, despite repeated requests; Levi Bendover polyester pants for women, when they were the top-selling pants across the nation; ET dolls, when the success of the movie put them on the top of every kid's Christmas list—and so on.

Somehow we allowed our self-image as fashion merchants to take precedence over the credo of satisfying our customers' wants and needs. We would find ourselves saying "That just isn't our customer."

THE FAR SIDE   By GARY LARSON

The Far Side cartoon by Gary Larson is reprinted by permission of Chronicle Features, San Francisco, CA. All rights reserved.

How Do You Define Customer?

When people tell you that they want to purchase goods or services from your business, can you, should you, dismiss them as not your customers? Strange idea, yet it happens all the time. An airline switched its first-class snack on short-hop flights from fresh fruit to high-quality, high-fat salted nuts, although they acknowledge that virtually 100 percent of their passengers have complained. Another airline, in its pre-boarding announcement, includes the startling statement that they do not count a "man's" briefcase as one of the two allowable carry-ons, leaving the businesswomen wondering if they are welcome or even visible.

How committed to serving you is the restaurant whose menu states "No changes or substitutions are allowed"? Of course, such an establishment probably also displays the customer-endearing sign: "Management reserves the right to refuse service to anybody."

Kenneth Stone, an economics professor from Iowa State University, specializes in consulting with local merchants threatened by the pending arrival of a national superstore. His advice is practical and effective: Focus product offerings and business practices more specifically on responding to customer needs. Across the country the findings are the same: If businesses would respond to the customers they already have rather than being concerned about responding to the threat of losing them, they could substantially improve both their revenues and their bottom lines.

A universal example is hours. Big stores generally keep longer hours than independent operators, and the small shop is pressured to compete. What about the customers' needs? Before being forced to be more flexible by the competition, local stores were often closed the very hours the customers had free to shop. Consider this example of a local hardware store. Before Wal★Mart opened with extended hours, the hardware store was closed from 2:00 p.m. Saturday through 10:00 a.m. Tuesday morning, and the rest of the week it closed every day at 5:00 p.m. By merely extending the hours

DILBERT reprinted by permission of UFS, Inc.

to accommodate the weekend and evening do-it-yourselfers and gardeners, business improved substantially—and held in the face of the new competition.

The idea that you know better than your customers what they really want and need can spring from an arrogance with innocent enough roots. A company with a history of pleasing the customer often forges ahead based on that history, rather than paying attention to the customers' current necessities and desires. Consider this commentary on Euro-Disney expressed in a recent *The Wall Street Journal* article.

> From impatient bus drivers to grumbling bankers, Disney stepped on toe after European toe. Former Disney executives shake their heads when they think about it, because much of Disney's attitude sprung, they say, from a relentless pursuit of quality, the very same drive for perfection that had made the company so successful.
>
> "We were arrogant," concedes one executive. "It was like, 'We're building the Taj Mahal and people will come—on our terms.' "[1]

IS THE CUSTOMER ALWAYS RIGHT?

"Yes." The customer is always right. But there are situations in which you clearly realize that what the particular person you are dealing with expects is not in the best interest of your company—or your other customers. Think of it as an implied contract.

The business commits to respect the customer and to provide the agreed-upon goods and services at the fairest price. The customer's responsibility is to respect the company and to demand only the level of goods and services for which he or she is willing to pay. The contract is broken when the customer's demands exceed the payment and endanger the company's ability to take care of other customers—or, in fact, to stay in business.

Loyal customers are the backbone of every company; rewarding that loyalty should be the focus of everyone's resources. Rewarding disloyalty is not providing a service to anyone. It encourages counterproductive behavior on the part of the nominal customer. It discourages people at every level in the company and makes them cynical about all customers. It depletes company resources and leaves less time, money, and energy for delighting the actual customers.

There is nothing a customer wants to hear more than "No problem! We can handle that." To foster that attitude in your company, you have to provide support for your people when they encounter that rare abusive customer. The best line of defense is strong management backing.

THE LAW OF UNINTENDED RESULTS

When you create policies, design products and services, or add business enhancements without soliciting input from your customers or monitoring their responses, you often squander resources and the customer's goodwill at the same time.

For example, the major airlines have developed compassionate policies designed to lessen a customer's financial burden when a loved one dies. The best of these

> ### The Half-Life of a Complaint[2]
>
> ♦ **4% of unhappy customers complain; 96% simply go away angry.**
>
> ♦ **For every customer complaint received, there are an average of 26 more people with problems; six of those are severe.**
>
> ♦ **Of those who complain, 56%-70% will do business with the company again, if the complaint is resolved. That goes up to 96% if it is resolved quickly!**
>
> ♦ **The average person who has a complaint tells 9-10 people about it. 13% tell more than 20 people.**
>
> ♦ **Customers whose complaints have been resolved, tell 5-6 people.**

policies is exemplified by Alaska Airlines: The bereaved relative flies to the funeral at the cheapest available rate.

The worst of these policies is probably also the most expensive to provide because it is an administrative nightmare. It is so laden with clauses and exceptions, it can leave the grieving passenger feeling misled at a very vulnerable time. It would be better if the airline simply announced that it had no compassionate fare.

A PRESCRIPTION FOR FABLED SERVICE

If you listen closely to customers who are delighted with the service they are receiving, you can develop the following simple prescription for fabled service: Believe that you are in business to serve customers, act on that belief, and the customers will respond.

Believe that you are in business to serve customers, act on that belief, and the customers will respond.

This prescription follows the pattern we have considered throughout this book: Each chapter ends with suggestions for reflection, or looking inward, and then with steps for putting beliefs into action.

The key to this prescription's effectiveness is that it guarantees customized service. If you treat your customers' expectations with the *respect* they deserve and respond with *flexibility*, you will provide service that maximizes your efforts and exceeds their expectations.

CUSTOMER VALUES

Just what are customers' expectations? Accepted service wisdom of the 1990s says that the customer is interested in three things: price, price, and price. A casual business observer might say that quality also plays an important role but is still suborned to the lowest price.

Prescription for Fabled Service

Ingredient #1: Respect

Make certain that every word and deed supports the belief that customers are the reason for your business.

Ensure that your people know that the litmus test for decision making is always: How will this affect our customers? Is this what the customers want and need?

Gather and filter all available input through direct feedback from customers, consultants, suppliers, service people, databases, and reports.

Ingredient #2: Flexibility

Develop a "have it your way" approach to the customers. All meaningful service guarantees, product warranties, and other assurances of customer satisfaction are based on flexible response. It isn't important that the customer abide by your rules. It is important that you have as few rules as possible and that all of those support reacting appropriately to your customers' needs.

Ensure that you are adapting to your customers' needs by getting decision making as close to the customer as possible. If there is a reason why the person who handles the customer directly cannot make decisions, reexamine that reason because it is probably misguided.

Give people on the front line both the authority and the responsibility to really take care of the customers. Your expectations mean everything. When you support your expectations with training and tools, you empower your staff. Customers feel best served when they have to deal with as few people as possible. There are no sweeter words, whether you are buying socks or negotiating a complicated lease, than "Don't worry—I'll take care of it." And there is nothing more frustrating than having to retell your story or repeat your request over and over again.

Business How-Tos for Serving Customers

Listen to what customers tell you about your business.

Involve the whole company in the service process.

Respect that customers vote most clearly with their patronage.

Benchmark yourself against winners (the ones the customers elect).

Hang out where your customers do.

Observe your customers using your products and services.

Relate your own experiences to your customers'.

Organize opportunities to pay attention (focus groups, employee site visits, the front line trained to listen and communicate feedback).

Create the customers' point of view for employees.

Does the preceding analysis begin to explain the real and lasting business successes of these times? Consider the following questions posed by Michael Treacy and Fred Wiersma in a *Harvard Business Review* article:

> How was Dell Computer able to charge out of nowhere and outmaneuver Compaq and other leaders of the personal computer industry? Why are Home Depot's competitors losing market share to this fast-growing retailer of do-it-your-self supplies when they are selling similar goods? How did Nike, a start-up company with no reputation behind it, manage to run past Adidas, a longtime solid performer in the sport-shoe market? All three questions have the same answers. First [these companies] redefined value for their customers in their respective markets. Second, they built powerful, cohesive business systems that could deliver more of that value than competitors. Third, by doing so they realized customers' expectations beyond the competition's reach. [3]

The authors of this study make the very convincing point that instead of considering value as being a simple combination of price and quality, customers today are looking for a level of customer intimacy, a degree of operational exellence, and an assurance of product quality. Successful companies have focused their efforts on excelling in the area where their customer places the most value, while making certain that they provide at least an acceptable level in the other two.

> *There isn't one standard set of service*
> *expectations that applies across the board.*

Consider the decisions you make as a customer, client, patient, or guest. Your choice of a fast-food restaurant or a Zagat restaurant guide's highest recommendation depends not only on price but also on whether you are looking for fast, dependable, inexpensive, reliable service (all related to operational excellence), or whether you are looking for personal recognition and attention, attention to detail, and ambiance (customer intimacy). Perhaps your main value when dining out is the creative reputation of the chef (product leadership).

The restaurants and companies that win your repeat patronage are those that correctly gauge what you most value about doing business with them and then set out to excel in that area while meeting acceptable benchmarks in the other areas.

This seems too obvious to be significant. Yet again, consider your own experiences as a customer. How many places where you do business seem to fully respect what you value and are obviously determined to be the very best at meeting your needs? Each of these elements represents service to customers: friendly, considerate personal treatment; a high level of operational efficiency; and impeccable product quality. There is a particular combination of these service elements, sometimes very narrow, sometimes a broad band, that represents what is most critical to the majority of your customers most of the time. The key is to recognize these customer values and to correctly gauge what

> *It is only when you exceed customers' expectations that they will give you credit for providing exceptional service.*

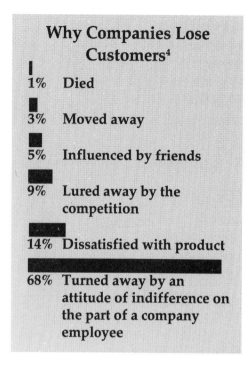

Why Companies Lose Customers[4]

1% Died

3% Moved away

5% Influenced by friends

9% Lured away by the competition

14% Dissatisfied with product

68% Turned away by an attitude of indifference on the part of a company employee

combination of them the customer expects from your business. If you will key into that combination by diligently trying to view your business from the customers' point of view, and then by continually refining your offer as your perceptions become clearer, you will fulfill your customers' expectations at a level well beyond the reach of your competition.

MOMENTS OF TRUTH AND OPPORTUNITY

Years ago, when he took over SAS and turned that failing airline around, Jan Carlzon, their president, made a significant contribution to our understanding of customer service. Of all of his wisdom, perhaps no bit is more useful for our consideration than the concept of "moments of truth."

A moment of truth is any interaction a customer has with our business.

The oft-quoted analogy Carlzon used to illuminate this concept was that of the dirty tray table: If a passenger finds that his tray table is not clean, he immediately makes assumptions about the attention paid to the jet engines.

What represents the equivalent of tray tables in your company? Besides the heart of the business transaction, what are the other points of relationship between your business and your customers?

Every personal interaction, every aspect of your operation, and the entirety of your product or service is considered and weighed against your customers' value systems. These are significant matters, and it is easy to understand their role in your customers' perceptions.

Seemingly little things matter too, however. In retail, management is reminded to enter their stores through the doors the customers use, to phone their switchboards, to receive shipments from their mailrooms, and to eat in their restaurants. Every part of the facility, every employee, and every product or process that bears the company's name reflect the level of respect you have for your customer. Each of these moments of truth, these contact points with the customers, need to be managed.

Everyone has heard a story similar to the one in which a casually dressed patron asked the bank to validate his parking. The teller snippily informed him that this was a perquisite of the bank's "good" clients. The customer calmly asked her to bring up his accounts, withdrew the million-plus dollars on deposit, and stepped across the street to become a good client of the bank's competitor.

> *Every part of the facility, every employee, and every product or process that bears the company's name reflect the level of respect you have for your customer.*

Reflect on some moment of truth that was the catalyst for your taking your business elsewhere. It may not have involved a tray table or a parking stub, but it probably was as insignificant in relation to the service as a whole. Your bank's officers or financial planners might be first rate, but a teller's inattention causes you to leave. Your favorite restaurant serves first-rate food, but the restroom is neglected.

The reasons customers leave may seem insignificant, but they are neither irrational nor unfathomable. They relate to the basic expectations everyone has when entering into a customer-supplier contract. How can you ensure that you and everyone in your company manage your business so that at every moment of truth the customer is served? Fortunately, if you believe that customers determine what service is, then there are some very definite steps you can take to ensure that the path to service excellence is clearly laid out for all your people to follow.

Jan Carlzon, SAS

Join Customers on the Job

There is no more reliable source of information about what the customer values than the customers themselves. Whatever the size of your business, regular interface with your customers could be one of the most productive uses of your time.

The most direct form of customer contact was characterized by Tom Peters as MBWA: Management By Walking Around. This was the form of customer contact practiced by Sam Walton, but it works in any business context. Sitting in on appointments, making sales calls, and attending important client meetings can all be enormously educational, as long as it is clear that you are there to learn, not to take over. Whether you attend a one-on-one meeting or a large gathering, your attentiveness will teach you a great deal about the customer and will communicate, to both your staff and customers, the priority in which you hold being of service.

Join Customers off the Job

You can continue your Management By Walking Around in your leisure time as well. Hang out where your customers hang out. Watch them use your products. You'll find yourself thinking of product applications that never occurred to you; you may even develop entirely new ones.

Many times, as people become more successful, they leave behind the middle class, which is the largest part of most markets. At one time the wealthiest man in America, Sam Walton insisted on a corporate culture that encouraged

associates to participate in, rather than disdain, the lifestyle of the customer. Corporate officers and directors dine at Denny's
and overnight at Motel 6, where they "keep
the light on for you." No matter how far up
the ladder anyone goes at the company,
they use Wal★Mart products and relate to
Wal★Mart customers' lifestyle. This keeps
the communication with the customer wide open.

The folks on the front lines—the ones who actually talk to the customer—are the only ones who really know what's going on out there.

ENCOURAGE CANDID INPUT

The reason you need to communicate to people company
wide that you value their feedback is painfully clear: As Sam
Walton is quoted in the Wal★Mart Associate Handbook,
"The folks on the front lines—the ones who actually talk to
the customer—are the only ones who really know what's
going on out there."[5]

In most companies, there is little reward in sharing
candid information about service with those who insulate
themselves from the truth. The willingness to hear it like it is
and to reward the messenger, rather than confuse him or her
with the message, will not only improve service, it will do
wonders for morale. A front line that is trained and rewarded
for listening and communicating up through the organization is a real point of difference for your company. Another
way to encourage staff to think like the customer is to send
people at every level out to visit the customers. What a
difference it makes to the accounting staff or to the inside
telephone sales department when they can meet customers
on a face-to-face basis.

RE-CREATE THE CUSTOMERS' REALITY

Ken Olsen, former chairman of Digital Equipment Corporation, a manufacturer of mini- and mainframe computers, had
a dramatic way of illustrating the impression that the company's product made when it arrived on the customer's

AP/Wide World Photos

Ken Olsen, former president of DEC, and John Sculley, former chairman of Apple Computer Inc.

loading dock. With crowbar in hand, Olsen would personally attempt to open the packing crates in front of large audiences of DEC employees. As they watched their chairman struggle with the crates, they got the message: This is what their customers were experiencing every time a DEC shipment arrived.

PRACTICE BEING A GOOD CUSTOMER

What is it that pleases you as a customer? When are you disappointed or downright angry? Stay attuned to your own service values and apply the golden rule to your customers.

The Neiman-Marcus retail chain, perhaps more than any other, denotes quality to the customer. Herbert Marcus' son and heir, Stanley Marcus, made a commitment that he would not buy anything that wasn't sold to him. He claimed a savings of almost $48,000 the first year he put his resolve into practice—a figure inflated somewhat by the BMW he didn't buy because the salesman was more interested in closing a deal than serving a customer.[6]

On reading about Mr. Marcus' commitment, I recognized his wisdom. If I were to lead good service in my own business, I had to establish strong personal standards for service. So I, too, set out to practice being a satisfied customer. Unfortunately, that saved me a lot of money too, even in Nordstrom stores. If I were interested in something and gave the sales staff every opportunity to make a sale but they still ignored me, then I either did without the item or hand carried it to another department or even to another branch where my patronage was appreciated. The expectation behind this simple relationship—if you care enough to sell it to me, I will

> The Neiman-Marcus retail chain was founded in 1907 by Herbert Marcus, Sr.; his sister Carrie Marcus Neiman; and her husband A.L. Nieman.

buy it—cannot be ignored. Try adopting this philosophy that you should not part with your money unless someone makes an effort to do more than merely take it from you and record the transaction. In doing so, you will learn a great deal about what it takes to make a customer feel valued. Thoughtful contemplation about your experiences will allow you to develop higher business standards. Conversely, if you do not exercise selectivity when your personal standards are compromised, you are liable to fall back on unconvincing preaching, rather than living out heartfelt practices.

CUSTOMERS VOTE WITH THEIR WALLETS

If you practice being a satisfied customer, you will confirm that customers vote with their wallets. All things being equal, the better the service, the better the sales. However you cut the business—departmentally, unit for unit, geographically, along product lines, or throughout the industry—sales are higher when customers are satisfied.

Fabled service is not some fuzzy approach to making people feel good. It is a realistic commitment to meeting the customers' real needs and winning their business.

BENCHMARK YOURSELF AGAINST THE BEST

Some critics claim that Wal★Mart is destroying retailing in small-town America.

> *No company's success can occur without*
> *the cooperation of the customer.*

If you are losing sales to a Wal★Mart in your industry, do not blame it on unfair business practices; instead, look carefully at what customers are telling you by their defection.

Given that customers vote with their wallets, winning companies are the ones that customers say yes to the most frequently. Don't confine competition for customers' dollars and the opportunity to learn more about what customers really want to your own industry. By exploring beyond expected boundaries you can develop meaningful insights into what would truly please your customers.

One oft-heard service disclaimer is that "Our customers don't expect that level of service." In discussing fallout related to their reorganization after filing for bankruptcy protection, a major department store noted that massive layoffs had made floor coverage somewhat skimpy, but the store downplayed the impact by saying, "...customers don't expect us to be like Nordstrom."

Does the other department store really believe that? If so, it is unfortunate for them, because customers do expect other retail stores to treat them as Nordstrom does. Being treated with respect and dignity by one company raises the standard everywhere, not just in the same environment or in comparable businesses. Customers tend to use their most satisfying experiences as their benchmark. What do you think your customers will expect of you if they have just been to Disneyland on a family vacation? Stayed at a Four Seasons Hotel? Eaten at an Olive Garden Restaurant? Renewed their policy with USAA? Of course customers of other stores expect them to be like Nordstrom! And so do yours.

Your customers will hold you to the highest standard. Use this reality to your advantage as you dedicate yourself to improving your business. There is only one Disneyland. If you are in the amusement park industry, benchmarking yourself against Disneyland will only allow you to stay in the race. It will not

Benchmarking Guidelines

1. **Identify your problems.**
2. **Choose organizations that are solving the problems you face.**
3. **Develop specific objectives before each visit.**
4. **Make the visit.**
5. **Debrief.**
6. **Convert learning to action.**
7. **Spread the learning throughout your organization.**
8. **Show the winners how much good has been done.**
9. **Repeat the cycle.**

Richard C. Whitely, The Customer-Driven Company. ©1991 by The Forum Corporation. Reprinted by permission of Addison-Wesley Publishing Company, Inc.

allow you to catch up or take home the trophy. However, if you are in a different business, it would truly be significant if you could become the Disneyland of that industry. Likewise, Nordstrom could leverage its strengths by benchmarking itself against Southwest Airlines and the Ritz-Carlton hotels. Another department store should not just imitate Nordstrom; instead it should study companies in other industries that exceed customer expectations. Find out who customers consider to be best in class and then measure yourself against those companies to improve service to your customers.

ONLY EXCEEDING CUSTOMER EXPECTATIONS QUALIFIES AS FABLED SERVICE

Do you need to be not only the best in your field but also the best overall? Yes, there is no alternative if you are truly committed to providing fabled service. Underestimating customer expectations will eventually lead to your demise. Meeting customer expectations will keep you in business, but you will always be at the mercy of fabled performers. Not only do your customers' expectations rise when they receive excellent service elsewhere, they rise when you raise the threshold of excellence in your business. You need to maintain a steadfast determination to provide service that is always better than expected—and better than your customers can get *anywhere* else.

Fabled service providers are not merely dedicated to providing good service; they are dedicated to exceeding their own standards. Fabled service providers are the original practitioners of continuous improvement.

> *"What can we do for them next?" is the operative question.*

Quite simply, there are no benchwarmer events in the service Olympics. There is no reward for resting on one's laurels.

That customers take service for granted is a given. The challenge, then, is to develop a reputation for a consistently high level of service that is punctuated with unexpected treats to delight the customers. Allowing room for the extraordinary is the key to fabled service leadership.

I mentioned the Ritz-Carlton earlier. Their motto is "Ladies and gentlemen serving ladies and gentlemen" and their courteous attentiveness is always a treat. What makes staying there a real pleasure however, are the small, unexpected things that they do. They present their frequent guests with a checklist and ask them to indicate personal preferences among all kinds of amenities. Then, in addition to the lovely, standard selection of room features, from time to time the Ritz-Carlton adds a very personal extra amenity. One time it might be a plate of fruit, another time it might be travel bags for shoes. Yet another time, it might be a special newspaper or magazine. How nice to check into your room and find something there meant just for you, when you least expect it.

Along the same lines, Hilton won my patronage forever by one night laying out a nightshirt on my bed. At first I thought that this was a loaner, but then I realized from the thoughtful note attached to it that I had indeed received a totally unexpected gift.

THE RITZ-CARLTON®
HOTEL COMPANY

Stop for a moment and think about how many ways there are to let a customer know how special he or she is. It's good business for the hotels to upgrade you to the nicest available room, no matter what you reserved. Or for the maitre d' to make a point of showing you to the best available seats. Or for the airline to upgrade you to the next class. What does each of these acts cost the companies? Those hotel suites would have been empty, those restaurant view tables unenjoyed, the better class airline seats unused. Does this mean that the customer will expect the suite for the price of a single or will never pay to fly at a higher level of class? Quite the contrary. Chances are that once your customers have experienced the best you have to offer, they will be more likely to ensure that they get it the next time by reserving it. The companies' deeds, not words, have told the customers that they are valued. You can rest assured that the customers will return the favor with their repeat business.

What makes service delightful? Unexpected. Undeserved. Unnecessary. These are service hallmarks that let customers know that the company really cares. Again, this level of service is only effective when it is on top of well-grounded day-in and day-out attention to the customers' needs. But it is the ingredient that makes all of our service efforts pay off. It is the leaven that raises the bread.

After one of many cross-country flights, I arrived home ready for bed, only to find my family, three hours fresher, ready for dinner. We decided to go to Fresh Choice, a restaurant that features a salad bar of eye- and palate-pleasing freshness, a variety of savory soups, several interesting pastas, fresh baked breads, and a dessert bar. Having spent the day exposed to airline food, I only wanted a little bit of hot soup to fill a very narrow void.

When I let the server behind the salad bar know my need, her friendly face darkened. "I'm so sorry," she said, and she did indeed look sorry. "We don't sell anything à la carte." Not normally larcenous, I realized that soup came with my family's meals and, since they weren't planning on having any, I decided to simply hitchhike on their fare. However, I was still mildly irritated that the restaurant had both soup and a customer who wanted to buy it, yet couldn't figure out how to make the sale.

Before I had a chance to get too grumpy, the server announced, "You are to be our guest. Enjoy all the soup you want, on the house!"

Delighters: Unexpected. Undeserved. Unnecessary. These are service hallmarks that let customers know that the company really cares.

We were all impressed and were discussing this great service when we arrived at the register. The man there was all smiles too. "No need to pay," he beamed. "You are our guests this evening." We tried to explain to him that actually only the soup was on the house, but in this case, the customers were wrong. The manager hurried out to tell us that, indeed, we were all to be guests that evening. Her words were memorable: "That's what Fresh Choice is all about. We can do anything we want whenever we want to make our customers happy. Tonight what we want to do is to let you be our guests on the house!"

We have returned to that restaurant often and share this story at every opportunity. It is important to review what makes this transaction significant. The restaurant is very satisfactory to begin with. The initial response to my need was disappointing, but not rude. The correction of the problem was delightful. The overcorrection was a mind blower; it was unexpected, unearned, and unnecessary. It was also the kind of service that is by definition fabled: service that customers talk about and turn into the standard.

GREAT COMPANIES CREATE AND NURTURE GREAT CUSTOMER RELATIONSHIPS

The sum of all of this is that companies and customers can enter into tacit covenants with each other that go far beyond the basic requirements of doing business together. Steven Covey uses a wonderful metaphor to describe the commitment great companies make to these relationships. He says you should treasure the goodwill of your customers as if it were a valuable account. Your goal is to always make deposits into that account, adding more than you ever take out and paying unexpected dividends. Treasuring your customers' goodwill is certainly a sound approach to building a lifetime covenant with them.

One phenomenon of American business in this century is the L.L. Bean Company, Inc. Originating in the otherwise obscure town of Freeport, Maine, this company has captured the hearts and reshaped the

buying patterns of America through its catalog sales. Buying
from a catalog can be a very impersonal venture, yet L.L.
Bean customers seem to cherish the illusion that they are
doing business with a very personal friend. What makes
them think that? Every aspect of L.L. Bean's business is
determined in response to customers' needs. It is a "user-
friendly" company, from its courteous, efficient handling of
orders, to its business hours (limited to 24 a day!) to its 100
percent satisfaction guarantee.

L.L.Bean®

Does it cost more to do business this way? In terms of
absolute costs, perhaps it costs more, but relative to the
revenues it creates, no. Adequate staffing,
giveaways, efficiency, and guarantees all
have price tags, but so do the inefficiencies
that come from providing services the customers don't care about. Or, worse yet, from
not providing opportunities for the customer to do business with you.

*T reasure the goodwill of your
customers as if it were a valuable
account. Your goal is to always
make deposits into that account,
adding more than you ever take
out and paying unexpected
dividends.*

**The real price tag in all
businesses is the terrible cost of
losing a customer.**

A serious *commitment* to the customer's definition of service
doesn't cost you anything, relative to the increase in revenues
such a commitment ensures.

Whatever else you do is insignificant if you haven't
tended to the basic relationship between your company and
your customers. Perhaps it is best summed up by the message on a simple sign that has been displayed in Nordstrom
stores for many years.

**The only difference between stores is how
we treat our customers.**

This truth is no less compelling for factories, offices,
practices, schools, brokerages, firms, hospitals, or whatever
term you use to describe your business.

REFLECTIONS

♦ If the customer doesn't care about it, it is not service.

♦ The foundation of legendary service is to believe that you are in business to serve the customer and then to act accordingly.

♦ In order to serve your customers, you must understand their values and consider how you are uniquely positioned to meet their needs.

♦ Every interaction your customers have with any aspect of your business creates a "Moment of Truth" in which they judge your commitment to their service—and make the decision whether or not to return.

♦ The best use of your time is being actively and responsively involved with your customers.

♦ Meeting expectations is required to be tolerated. Exceeding expectations is required to be fabled.

♦ Unexpected. Undeserved. Unnecessary. Service that makes the difference is in the margins.

♦ The only difference among companies is in how we treat our customers.

ACTION STEPS

Question all of your business precepts. Weigh what you do against what your customers say you should do. Now.

>   Develop a simple system to elicit constant feedback.

>   Involve front-line employees in information gathering.

>   Ask open-ended questions; accept responses seriously—and gratefully.

>   Incorporate what you learn from customers into strategies.

>   Respond personally to all suggestions and criticisms.

Underpromise and overdeliver.

Keep decision making as close to the customer as possible.

Analyze business from your customers' perspective: use your products and services; visit your locations.

Commit to continuous improvement. Always surpass your best performance, as each experience sets a new benchmark for the customer.

*C*ommitment:
To Serve Those
Who Serve the Customer

◆ Understand your role

◆ Focus on what your people need

◆ Share your mission, values, and goals

◆ Make work meaningful

◆ Give people the freedom and support to be their best

Fabled Service Is Everyone's Job

4

What transforms slave-like labor into exalted service are
the amount of skilled required to provide it;
the importance of the need or desire served;
the relationship between the server and the served;
and prevailing religious, moral, and social opinion.

Russell L. Ackoff

The Issue

In every organization dealing with the public, there are only two job descriptions: An employee either supports the customers directly, or supports the people who do. This gives rise to two key principles of providing fabled service: Everyone works for the external customers, whether directly or indirectly, and nobody gets a paycheck unless those customers are well cared for.

Furthermore, each person in the organization performs a service for somebody else. No one is too important; no one is too insignificant. Service is beyond no one, and no job is too menial. Service, then, is a continuum, with everyone focused on assuring customer care.

Two Job Descriptions

There is a great deal of emphasis today on the importance of reengineering business processes to maximize people and resources. In the fabled service organization, there are really only two kinds of people:

1. The front-line people who directly take care of the customers.
2. All subsequent levels who take care of the front-line people.

In successful companies, a continuum of care exists from the entry-level position to the executive suite and back around again. No job is too menial and no job is too important.

Consider this sobering reality:

Your lowest-paid, shortest-tenured, entry-level employee generally has more interaction with the customer than you do.

Think of "The Happiest Place on Earth," for example. Michael Eisner and the late Frank Wells did a masterful job in leading Disney into the 1990s, yet how many visitors to the Disney parks have the slightest awareness of these much-heralded executives? Instead, the customers' impression of the company is much more likely to come from the street sweeper who cheerfully gives them directions or from the senior citizen who takes their tickets and welcomes them to the park.

To lead your people to fabled service, you must serve them well by hiring the right people, providing meaningful work, preparing them well for their jobs, giving them ongoing support, and then, finally, by getting out of their way.

As an executive, my relative importance to Nordstrom customers was revealed to me one evening as I stood at a store exit wishing the departing shoppers a good evening. This had been an extraordinarily successful first day of a major sales event; we had broken all previous records. Like the rest of the crew, I was wearing the uniform of the day: a green polo shirt, white pants, and comfortable running shoes.

The last customers left long after closing had been announced, staggering under their bags full of bargains. Unable to contain my exuberance, I bantered with them, expressing my condolences that they had not been able to find anything that they liked. As they walked out the door, one woman turned to her companion and remarked, "What in the world do they do to these people? Even the doorman is happy!"

A happy door attendant was much more impressive to them than a happy executive. What more concrete evidence do customers have of the company's total commitment to service than the care with which the door attendants, janitors, and delivery people do their jobs?

LEADING YOUR PEOPLE

There is probably no organization today that does not firmly articulate its commitment to the customer, either as part of its mission statement or as a prime goal. What sets apart the companies providing fabled service is their clear understanding of everyone's responsibility to serve the customer.

Some do so directly. This is easy to understand. What becomes more difficult to understand is that those who serve the customer indirectly can only do so by serving someone else in the organization directly.

Thus, in a distributorship, the retailer serves the end customer. The distributor serves the retailer. The wholesaler serves the distributor. The factory serves the wholesaler. The raw materials supplier serves the factory.

Within the distributorship itself, the sales force serves the retail customer; sales support and sales management serve the sales force; distribution, advertising, and operations serve that sales support level; and the executives serve the functional support.

The system breaks down most frequently at either end of the typical hierarchy. Someone at the bottom of the heap has no sense of how his job impacts the mission, so he does it sloppily, or he does not show up, and the integrity of the process is thrown off.

Or, the person at the top has grown beyond needing to focus on the customer. Busy with the board, with stock analysis, and other executive-level responsibilities, he is unavailable to his management team and completely out of touch with the actual customers.

Service is an ongoing, continual process throughout the organization. Therefore, everything we say about taking care of the customers applies to every one in the organization, from hiring through empowering.

ENSURING SERVICE IS EVERYONE'S JOB

The mystery is why so few companies distinguish themselves by the excellence of their employees at every level. The key is squarely in the hands of management. If we can focus our efforts on setting up an environment in which our employees can succeed, they will drive even our loftiest visions far beyond our highest expectations. What is required from us is vision, attention, communication, and trust.

HIRE RIGHT

Over the years, I have been asked repeatedly how to hire wonderful people and what type of employee training guarantees success. My candid response? Hire nice people whose parents trained them well.

If you hire the wrong people, your vision will be dashed at every turn. You simply cannot make "not nice" people want to treat the customers—and each other—well. As difficult as it is to define, you have to hire people with the right attitude because it cannot be trained, mandated, or motivated into being.

A humorous statement attributed to a man named Paul Dickson sums it up well:

> ***Never try to teach a pig to sing. It wastes your time and it annoys the pig.***

We are all guilty of trying to make divas out of porkers, or, to use the more familiar aphorism, of trying to make silk purses out of sows' ears. If you want service in your company, hire people who possess a great attitude about service. No matter how brilliantly qualified the person is in other areas, if he or she does not want to be of service to customers—internal or external—you are sabotaging your efforts. The standard has to be clearly set and adhered to if service is to be dynamic.

Even if you are not involved in hiring and training the people in your company, your strong leadership in these areas is imperative if you want everyone to understand and reflect your values. Again, your role is to serve those who serve the customers. How can you support the hiring process so that your company employs people with the potential to succeed on the job?

Expect Each Job to Be Well Defined

Hiring right means carefully defining the job to be filled. What characteristics are possessed by people who are successful in that job? Are you systematically trying to find people with similar characteristics to add to the staff? As elementary as this may seem, it is seldom practiced.

It is instructive to read the want ads. It seems that no matter what position is advertised, the qualifications include a college degree and a specified amount of related experience. Certain characteristics are deemed desirable: self-starter, responsible, flexible, and so on. There is nothing wrong with any of these requirements, but what do they have to do with the job at hand? Do any of these qualities help you

In 1901 a hard-working Swedish immigrant named John W. Nordstrom took a small stake from the Klondike gold rush and opened a store in Seattle. Today, his descendants are the proud proprietors of 75 fashion stores in 10 states, with plans for strong, continued growth.

to find people with the passion and the grit to satisfy the customer?

Consider the ad Nordstrom ran when it opened a brand new store in a territory where the population had never heard of them before. Many years ago, a salesperson in Spokane noticed a "Salesperson Wanted" ad posted in a shop window. Its message was so profound that the employee copied it. We used a variation when we sought staff for our first California store and in subsequent employment advertisements for several years thereafter. The wording went something like this:

> WANTED: PEOPLE POWER
> We are looking for people to work with us on our new venture.
> People to sell, and people to take care of salespeople.
> People to lead and people to follow.
> People to work hard and to take pride in their work.
> People who respect themselves and enjoy others.
> People who are honest, industrious, caring and dedicated.
> People who want to succeed and want others to succeed, too.
> People with vision and with the determination to live their vision.

What would constitute "People Power" at your company? Your list of qualifications might well be different. The point is the qualifications you include should relate specifically to the characteristics necessary to succeed at the job at hand and should never be merely a list of standard credentials. If a degree has nothing to do with the job requirements, don't make it a criterion. If prior experience is difficult to qualify and may, in fact, have encouraged bad habits, don't establish it as an arbitrary barrier.

On the other hand, as important as it is not to establish extraneous qualifications, it is absolutely essential to search for those people who *do* have the qualifications you need. The

Nordstrom People Power ad, for example, makes no bones about the imperatives: hard working, dedicated, people loving, honest, caring...the picture is vivid and accurate.

Expect Every Employee to Work Well With People

Apply the same standards to the interview process as you did to the classified ads. Encourage your people to look for qualities that are directly related to the job at hand. No matter what your business, some sense of collegiality is necessary. Everyone your company hires needs to work well with people: customers, fellow employees, or, in most cases, both. Therefore, encourage the interviewers to be sensitive to their gut reactions.

Expect Every Employee to Work With Your Customers

To ensure that employees take service to the customer seriously, insist that, despite the ultimate job assignment, everyone's initial stint be one that involves face-to-face customer contact. This works particularly well if promotions are contingent upon showing an aptitude for customer care. This approach supports the company's commitment to service in two important ways.

- ♦ It gives the employee a clear indication of the company's true level of commitment to the customer.

- ♦ As employees move through the company, they never lose empathy with the front line they will be supporting.

Wal★Mart attempts to give everyone it employs an opportunity to come face-to-face with the customer. For instance, the corporation's busy buyers are required to spend time in the Wal★Mart stores on a regular basis as part of a program called "Eat What You Cook." During this period, they try to sell the merchandise they selected, which looked so good in the showroom, directly to the customers. In addition, they step into the shoes of the department manager and are challenged to handle the processing and presentation of all the merchandise they have bought for a particular store.

The Mission of Southwest Airlines

The mission of Southwest Airlines is dedication to the highest quality of Customer Service delivered with a sense of warmth, friendliness, individual pride, and Company Spirit.

To Our Employees

We are committed to provide our employees a stable work environment with equal opportunity for learning and personal growth. Creativity and innovation are encouraged for improving the effectiveness of Southwest Airlines. Above all, employees will be provided the same concern, respect, and caring attitude within the organization that they are expected to share externally with every Southwest Customer.

At Southwest Airlines, legend has it that you never know who will be on the plane serving the customer, as various members of senior management have been known to experience the business firsthand. Rumor has it that if the attendant is particularly funny and friendly, he is probably Herb Kelleher, chairman of the board.

PROVIDE MEANINGFUL WORK

Once hired, what is it we expect people to do? Companies that have distinguished themselves through their service have no monopoly on conscientious, reliable people. However, fabled service companies provide an environment in which people can fully develop their aptitude for service. If everyone hires, retains, and promotes people with reference to fundamental service standards, the point of difference is a beneficial climate that allows the provision of service to thrive at every level.

ServiceMASTER has long been admired and emulated for its service practices. One of their credos is especially insightful in the area of encouraging extraordinary levels of performance from each and every person: Before you ask people to do something, you have to help them to be something.

The desire for a meaningful life is not limited to those who are better educated, more traveled, more highly compensated, or at a higher level of responsibility. If you respect the basic dignity of each person in your organization and ascribe to each the desire to make a difference, they will revolutionize your company. Quite simply, most people are capable of contributing far more than you ever elicit.

There is a well-known fable about the man who came upon three people working.

> "What are you doing?" he asked the first. "I am cutting stone," the fellow replied. "And miserable work it is too." To the same question, the second person said, "I am supporting my family. It's no joy, but at least we eat." The third man's face lit up when the question was posed to him. "What am I doing?" he responded with a lilt in his voice. "Why, I am building a great cathedral, which will stand forever more as a tribute to the glory of God and a monument to man's goodness. The work is a joy and the reward is beyond measure."

*B*efore you ask people to do something, you have to help them to be something.

Our Vision

To be an ever expanding and vital market vehicle for use by God to work in the lives of people as they serve and contribute to others.

*Service*MASTER.

Provide Opportunity for Authentic Participation

Most of the work that people perform is not as arduous as hewing stone, but it can be every bit as tedious; it is transformed when the worker believes that it is meaningful. In the Nordstrom, Inc., 1990 Annual Report, salesperson Ann Hansen shares her view of her job: "Selling is not a learned thing; it's a God-given talent. This is my gift. It's my hobby, it's my talent, it's what I do best."

There is no greater privilege in life than being served by people who love what they do because what they do is meaningful. We expect to find this attitude among those who are doing things of great significance. We are delighted and humbled to find it among those relating to us or caring for our needs, from simple to complex. When the people who take care of us demonstrate that they believe they are involved in a worthwhile activity, we define the service they provide as fabled.

In order to elevate the daily business of your company to a meaningful level you need to foster participation in the fundamentals of the company. Max De Pree was the chairman of Herman Miller, a furniture company whose dedication to the customer certainly makes it legendary by virtually anyone's standards. Mr. De Pree analyzed the fundamental characteristic of exceptional companies as follows:

> Modern corporations should be communities, not battlefields. At their hearts lie covenants between executives and employees that rest on shared commitment to ideas, to issues, to values, to goals, and to management processes. Words such as love, warmth, personal chemistry are certainly pertinent.[1]

Engage Everyone From Vision to Reality

Let's focus on how to facilitate this shared commitment to values, goals, and management processes. Essentially, your people—at every level—need to be involved in finding the answers to the following four questions, each of which builds on the previous:

♦ Why are we in business?

♦ What do we believe in?

♦ Where are we going?

♦ How do we get there?

Mission: Why Are We in Business?

This is the fundamental question to ask of any endeavor: Why are we doing this? Interestingly, you know the answer to this. Quite probably you have immortalized it on a plaque in twenty-five words or less.

Unfortunately, well-wrought words, even when etched in concrete, do not make a mission statement. That statement is made by the constant, shared redefining of the *why* of the business. For others to share in your success, they, too, must be able to internalize the significance of what it is you are about. The answer to this question must be clear, candid, constantly communicated, and dynamic.

The formulation of this mission has a marked effect on how you carry out your business. Never lose sight in the last analysis that sales are the outcome of service. If you respond to "why are we in business?" with "to take care of our customers' widget needs," rather than "to sell X number of widgets at Y return," you will set a whole different approach to your business in the process.

> *T o be successful, you have to have your heart in your business and your business in your heart.*
> —Thomas Watson, Sr.

To be a mission, the reason for being in business should be highly charged. Think of the strength of mission as in "missionary zeal." That is the fervor each of your people could have for your business, with you leading the charge. Again, think of Leon Royer's wonderful term, "monomaniac with a mission." Does that begin to describe the model you provide to the rest of the company?

Values: What Do We Believe In?

The second question is "what do we believe in?" What qualities provide the standards by which we measure our success? What is bedrock for us in good times or in times like these? (By definition, times are never good, except in retrospect!)

This is not a rhetorical question with an obvious answer. The values that you sincerely espouse will inform every decision and determine every course of action. You need to clearly communicate what those values are, in deed as well as in word, or you will develop a culture of cynicism, rather than enthusiasm.

The late founder of McDonald's, Ray Kroc, was clear from the start about the values that defined his company: quality, service, cleanliness, and value. He built these qualities into every part of the system.

It is amazing to go into McDonald's today, in any part of the world, and find that the founder's values are being adhered to by people who never even knew him or might not even know his name. If there is any form of immortality, it might be found in the long life of values that are passionately held and shared.

An open discussion of companywide values enlists the support of others to help you practice what you preach. Furthermore, you attract people who share your values, which creates a powerful force for building and maintaining a successful business.

Vision: Where Are We Going?

Where do you see yourself in the near future? Planning for the future does not assure complete control over what will happen next, but it is a surefire way to energize what is happening now.

Theodore Hesburgh, the legendary president of Notre Dame, noted that

> The very essence of leadership is, you have to have a vision. It's got to be a vision you articulate clearly and forcefully on every occasion. You can't blow an uncertain trumpet.[2]

Employees look to you for leadership on the question of "where are we heading?" At the same time, their close-to-the-customer experience can provide invaluable input as the answer evolves. Encouraging everyone to share the vision and to become involved in its ongoing refinement is the essence of truly empowering the organization.

> *As you support possibility thinking, you not only raise the bar of what the company can achieve, you raise the level of aspiration for each individual.*

Napoleon observed that "...a leader is a dealer in hope." Sam Walton, in reflecting on the unforeseeable growth his company had experienced, commented: "I had no vision of the scope of what I would start. But I had confidence that as long as we did our work well and were good to our customers, there would be no limit to us."[3]

Strategic Goals: How Do We Get There?

Goal setting becomes strategic when it arises out of the honest and constant reevaluation of where you are headed and why. Gazing into your crystal ball makes no strategic sense. In a typically trenchant observation, Peter Drucker reminds us that "Strategic planning is necessary precisely because we cannot forecast...Strategic planning does not deal with future decisions. It deals with the futurity of present decisions."[4] In other words, we can only assure our futures by integrating all of our resources to assure our present.

Good enough never is, and better is only acceptable if there is commitment to make it best. When dealing with the customer, you are only as good as your last encounter.

People at every level of the organization have valid insights into what resources are available and how best to deploy them. They will be particularly valuable participants in determining what it will take to achieve your vision, but only if they have been involved in forming that vision. As the leader, your commitment to share your deliberations on these issues and to invite and integrate participation is part of a process. It cannot be episodic and it cannot be routine. It needs to be lively, challenging, and completely involving.

DRIVING THE VISION, MAKING THE GOALS

Maintain High Standards

Leaders of successful companies involve everyone in understanding why they are in business and then in planning how to move that business forward. Thus, if everyone is responsible for service, everyone has to be held to high standards. Never apologize for demanding the best from your people.

Standards have to be absolute. The execution of those standards can be as personal and varied as the people involved, but customers and employees alike must always know what to expect. Good enough never is, and better is only acceptable if there is commitment to make it best.

When your customer evaluates your service, it is only as good as your last encounter. It does not seem fair that your customer can eat in your restaurant for years, but the first time she encounters slow or surly service she stops being a regular. This is true of every business: You invite the customer back with each transaction. If everybody in the company serves customers, there can be no slack cut when it comes to excellence. There is no area where toleration of sloppiness will not result in decreased service quality.

It is these very high standards that allow fabled companies to win their customers' allegiance. Everyone likes to be associated with winners. If everyone is held to high standards, then no one will be embarrassed by anybody on the team. The expectation of excellence causes everyone to stretch, and the customer is well served in the process.

An Environment in Which to Prosper

You want people who are going to cast their lot with you. You want to inspire them to stretch to their utmost and, in turn, to inspire you to grow. You want them to serve your customers as well as you attempt to serve them. All this being true, you have to pay them more than lip service.

An Environment in Which to Grow

People who are part of a team that is successfully building a strong service organization find themselves hotly sought after by other companies. Ironically, these are often the hardest people to pry loose, no matter how lucrative the offer, as they are motivated by the intangible, yet deeply satisfying, challenges and rewards of being associated with a winner.

At one point, someone informed Bruce Nordstrom that a prestigious company was trying to woo me away from Nordstrom. In the course of an otherwise casual lunch conversation, he asked me what it was going to take to finally shake my commitment. Without considering my response, I answered from my gut. I assured him that I would never leave Nordstrom as long as I was making a contribution. If the time came when I was no longer making a contribution, I hoped I would recognize it long before anyone else did.

My comments, coming some ten years into my career, surprised me. I had never before considered why I regularly turned down opportunities offering multiples of my current salary and important-sounding titles. I had a tremendous responsibility at Nordstrom, and I was expected to grow along with it. This freedom and responsibility to grow gave me the most challenging career opportunity I could envision. In recognizing that drive in myself, I was stimulated to

> **People are self-motivated and only need from management[5]**
>
> ♦ To be well prepared for the job
> ♦ To have unnecessary and demeaning barriers removed
> ♦ To have achievements recognized

support the same kind of growth in the others on my team. Who knows if we had the quantifiably best people? Having people working to be their best gave us an unassailable qualitative advantage.

EMPOWERMENT

"Empowerment" would surely head the list of most overused terms in the past decade. This is unfortunate, for empowered people take their responsibility for pleasing the customers seriously. The secret of empowerment is sharing the responsibility, the authority, and the resources necessary for success with the appropriate people.

It is virtually impossible to oversee service as it occurs during "moments of truth." It is a real-time process that usually occurs away from the watchful eyes of management. There is no control over its circumstances. The key to providing fabled service is to get decision making done as close to the customer as possible. This means that you have to entrust your customers to the front-line, entry-level people—and you have to equip these people to do the job.

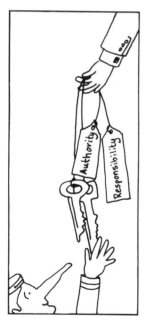

John Nordstrom's one-page commitment to empowerment is reproduced on the next page. There is only one rule at Nordstrom:

Use your good judgment in all situations.

The handbook reflected a very real and positive commitment to the employees' ability to make good decisions, which has been a part of the Nordstrom culture for three generations.

Empowered to use their good judgment, people at all levels of Nordstrom come up with solutions to problems, improvements to processes, and other ideas that are as timely as they are creative. When a customer responds to the great service, it is a reaction to an employee who takes responsibility for his or her satisfaction right there on the spot. There

WELCOME TO
NORDSTROM[6]

We're glad to have you with
our company.

Our number one goal is to provide
outstanding customer service.

Set both your personal and
professional goals high.
We have great confidence in your
ability to achieve them.

Nordstrom Rules:

Rule #1: **Use your good
judgment in all situations.**

There will be no additional rules.

Please feel free to ask your department manager,
store manager, or division general manager
any questions at any time.

NORDSTROM

is an "absolutely no-problem attitude" on the part of Nordstrom salespeople; they take the challenge of sending the
customer away delighted very seriously.

This level of empowerment only occurs where the respect for everyone's commitment and ability is genuine. To
achieve this is a worthwhile challenge to your leadership.
There is no substitute. It cannot be faked. On many occasions,
I have observed companies pouring time, money, and energy
into getting their front line to "be like Nordstrom" or to "out
Disney Disneyland" or to "be more hospitable than Marriott"
or to "be more reliable than McDonald's." I know with

I like the freedom. It's like I have my own little business—my own men's store.
Charles McGlothlin:
Tysons Corner, VA

I don't always have to go to the boss for a decision. I can do what I think is right for the customer.
Carol Enderson:
Northgate, WA

It's amazing how many resources the company provides for employees. It's like your own little business. Everything is provided for you, all you have to do is go out there and work hard.
Danny Galos:
Santa Ana, CA

I like the idea that they give me the flexibility to run the department the way I think it ought to be run, with good business sense.
Joan Shenk:
Tysons Corner, VA

(Being an entrepreneur means...) having the freedom to make decisions— to do whatever I feel is necessary to satisfy my customer. There are no limitations.
Mary Goins:
Horton Plaza,
San Diego, CA

certainty that all is for naught when they exhibit the disregard they have for "those people out there on the firing line." One CEO, after an eighteen-month program to improve service, struggled to label his salespeople and, in attempting to avoid "clerks," hit upon the euphemism "the little people." The little people???!!! If little people are serving your customers, your business is doomed.

Contrast this with Sam Walton's insight: "If you want a successful business, your people must feel that you are working for them—not that they are working for you."[7]

OWNERSHIP: SERVICE IS EVERYONE'S JOB

It seems that every opportunity to focus business on customers exposes the same dynamic—empowerment. Empowerment denotes filling with power and connotes enriching, enlarging, and inspiring.

Empowering employees

♦ Turns them on to their potential, if supported by the company's resources

♦ Allows them to be their best, to try their hardest, to explore all avenues

♦ Encourages them to take reasonable risks and to make sound judgments

♦ Permits them to learn from their mistakes and grow

You have committed to designing quality into every aspect of your business. The result of these efforts is the empowerment that you share with your people and that they accept.

The 1990 Nordstrom, Inc., Annual Report is a manual on service leadership. It highlights the stars—those people who were chosen for the job, trained, supported, and then energized by the opportunity and the expectation to take care of the customers. They are quoted here.[8]

REFLECTIONS

♦ If service at your company is to be legendary, it must be everybody's business.

♦ There are two job descriptions: Those who take care of customers and those who take care of caretakers.

♦ Your expectations of the people who serve the customer: Good judgment, positive attitude, passion for the customer, desire to be part of a winning team, willingness to give their all.

♦ Your people's expectations of you: All of the above, plus meaningful work, respect, the opportunity to share the big picture, a clear set of standards, ongoing training, appreciation and recognition, responsibility for decisions, freedom and support to be their best.

ACTION STEPS

Ask yourself how you can better serve the needs of your direct customers, so that they can do the same for their customers.

Make certain there are no jobs labeled "Customer Service." Service is everyone's job.

Get to know the people at all levels of your company—and allow them to get to know you.

Be alert to what makes you a happy customer, then apply what you learn to your company.

Equip your people to deliver fabled service: Share the vision, train them in the basics, provide them with all of the necessary tools, give them feedback, get out of their way.

Commitment:
To Design Every Part of Your Business With Service As the Desired Outcome

---

♦ Develop all systems with service in mind

♦ Make it simple for customers to do business with you

♦ Think through all processes deploying resources: human, material, financial

♦ Instill the thrill of service

Fabled Service
Is Designed Into
the System

At the core of every great customer service organization is a package of systems and a training program to inculcate those programs into the soul of that company.

Ken Blanchard and Sheldon Bowers

5

The Issue

Most businesses do not give much thought to customers when systems are designed. This oversight is apparent to customers, who, given the choice, do business with organizations that do consider their needs in every stage of planning and that constantly readjust their systems to meet changing customer needs.

Again, it is critical to recognize that every interaction between a customer and the company is a *Moment of Truth*. Each Moment of Truth gives your customer a definite impression of your commitment to service. Therefore, carefully plan each aspect of your business, then follow through and always measure and analyze the results.

Managing interactions is not the same as managing things. Since the outcome of a customer interaction is totally in the hands of each service provider, the system should be designed to support and enhance these individual interactions. In general, the fewer systems the better; all should be designed to get decision making as close to the customer as possible. Finally, the design and planning of training must be as well thought out as the design of the computer system.

WHY CAN'T YOU FIND GOOD PEOPLE?

One day, after a meeting to discuss some United Way issues, the chairman of the area's largest retailer brought up our mutual business. "I still think you must import your people from the Northwest," he challenged. "We simply can't find the people here in Southern California to do the job."

The next morning the chairman's company ran an eight-page section in the *Los Angeles Times* advertising the "biggest-ever" White Sale. Since both of my then-teenaged sons wanted new sheets—zebra-striped sheets to be exact—I decided to do some shopping and research at the same time.

I was challenged to analyze the situation so that I never made the mistake of taking the quality of our people for granted. More to the point, I was fairly certain that the differences would be found not in the caliber of the people, but in the caliber of the management support, and I had no intention of taking that for granted either. Sure enough, the opportunities for improvement were obvious. I arrived as the store opened, and I was not alone.

Obviously, the store's advertising was doing its job of attracting customers. What then was causing the salespeople to be unproductive? Let me share with you what I observed:

♦ There were only two salespeople on the very large floor to handle the response generated by eight pages of compelling advertising.

- One salesperson was a trainee, evidently in her first day on the job, who didn't do much more than shadow the already harried other salesperson.

- Only one of two cash register stations was open.

- The telephone was located at the closed station and the phone system did not allow for remote pick-up. Every time the phone rang, the salespeople stopped whatever they were doing and ran to answer it.

- The department was in a shambles—merchandise in disarray, cartons blocking aisles, and litter carpeting the floor.

- The merchandise was not organized. If I had not been looking for an easy-to-spot pattern, I would have given up. As it was, it took me an annoying amount of time to find all of the sizes and pieces that I needed. Other shoppers were muttering to themselves, looking around vainly for help, then walking out.

- There was a long, slow-moving line at the single open cash register. None of the merchandise was ticketed, so every piece's style number had to be looked up in its own vendor book, then hand keyed into the terminal. With dozens of vendors and a couple thousand styles, this was a tedious process.

- The salespeople were shabbily dressed and poorly groomed. Their very demeanor was menial, in keeping with their minimum hourly pay rate.

YOUR PEOPLE ARE ONLY AS GOOD AS YOUR SYSTEMS

If it isn't obvious to the customers, it is irrelevant.

Clearly, the difference between Nordstrom salespeople and the other store's salespeople was in the systems that supported them. The hiring pool was the same. The tangible differences are attributable to the training, support, technology, tools, goals, and rewards that define the environments in which these people are expected to work.

Where do you find people to serve the customer well? Everywhere and anywhere. The challenge is to build good service into all of your systems so that your people can do their jobs.

In the White Sale example, which systems were flawed?

♦ Merchandise handling

♦ Ticketing

♦ Pricing

♦ Voice communications

♦ Scheduling

♦ Training

♦ Compensation

THE FAR SIDE   By GARY LARSON

Inconvenience stores

The advertising to support the White Sale cost the company an estimated one hundred thousand dollars. The company succeeded in luring people into the stores, only to discourage customers through inefficient systems and, thus, to lose sales. Senior management undoubtedly blamed the disappointing sales on a combination of poor advertising and inadequate employees. That assessment fails to uncover the systemic causes of the mediocre performance, which, if addressed, would unleash the full potential of their people.

There is an old saying that it would behoove us all to commit to memory—and learn in our hearts: *The front line can't lie.* This means, quite simply, that the superstructure you can see accurately reflects the infrastructure that supports it.

Again, one of the reasons that the retail industry provides a fertile ground for learning about the basics of service is that it is so transparent to customers. Thus, you can observe what works and doesn't work from your personal perspective as a customer, then apply these learnings to your own business. It is ironic that the chairman of a major retailer had tried to find a formula, when all he needed to do was spend some thoughtful time in his own stores.

The difference lies not so much in the people, but in the management.

Different Strategies

At Nordstrom, the focus for a special sale would be on the planning and execution. Staffing would be beefed up to provide additional coverage for the anticipated business. All terminals would be open, and additional facilities would be set up to quickly process customers' purchases. Extra dressing rooms would be installed in appropriate departments.

A percentage of the money otherwise spent on advertising would be applied to making customers happy that they had responded to the sale. This would also assure that customers came back. For example, at its legendary Half-Yearly or Anniversary sales, Nordstrom offers complimentary valet parking, and complimentary means what it says. Gratuities are cheerfully refused by parking attendants. If a sale occurs during a rain shower, store personnel accompany shoppers to and from their vehicles under umbrellas. As a customer, you can easily recognize the differences in such a systematic approach to business.

Major Customer Turnoffs

- ◆ **Desired merchandise out of place, out of stock, on order**
- ◆ **Help not available when it is needed**
- ◆ **Employees who are poorly trained, uninformed, or distracted**
- ◆ **Bureaucratic processes and red tape**
- ◆ **Waiting: in line, on the phone, anytime...**
- ◆ **Prices not clearly marked**
- ◆ **Misleading advertising**
- ◆ **Value not commensurate with price paid**
- ◆ **Quality that doesn't live up to expectations**
- ◆ **Failure to stand behind products or services**
- ◆ **Poor housekeeping: dirt, disorder, safety hazards**
- ◆ **Inconvenient: location, layout, parking, access**

Service has to be a forethought, not an afterthought. Build service into all parts of your operation from the beginning, rather than frustrating yourself, your people, and your customers by trying to engineer it along the way.

If we truly dedicate ourselves to instill that thrill of merchandising—the thrill of buying and selling something at a profit—into every one of our associate-partners, nothing can ever stop us. That means that you have the merchandise the customer wants, when the customer wants it, and you make it easy to buy it.

Sam Walton

Whatever your business, customers value some combination of the following:

♦ Genuine courtesy
♦ Quality: People, Product, Process
♦ Efficiency
♦ Effectiveness

Having what the customer wants and making it easy for the customer to buy it: These simple concepts define the basis of good business. While the validity of this advice is intuitively obvious, its application is rare enough that it gives a strong competitive advantage to those who do apply it.

Service, although often dismissed as the soft side of management practice, is the issue. All of your systems must be designed and executed to ensure that you have what the customers want, when they want it. *This* is when fabled companies focus on the management of service. The moments of truth and the points of purchase are occurrences that take place outside the direct purview of management. The management of these events comes in the careful planning and execution of all supporting elements of the business related to satisfying the customer.

Service has to be a forethought, not an afterthought. Build service into all parts of your operation from the beginning, rather than frustrating yourself, your people, and your customers by trying to engineer it along the way.

Many years ago, Peter Drucker caught my attention when he observed that most of what we call management today consists of getting in the way of the people doing the work. The key to great service management is to provide a way to support solid decision making as close to the customer as possible.

*The hallmarks of systems that scale
the highest peaks of service are simplicity
and relevance.*

Fortunately, there are many opportunities to refine systems
so they serve your customers—and you.

DESIGN THE
ORGANIZATION

Does the structure of your organization support the delivery of service?

Frances Hesselbein, longtime
chief executive officer of the Girl
Scouts of America, has earned a
reputation for leadership excellence.
Among her many contributions to
the art and science of management is
the unique structure that Hesselbein
developed to support the dynamics
of her organization.

Hesselbein conceived the corporation she led to be organized in a
series of concentric circles. Her position was in the innermost circle,
which was surrounded by a circle
representing her management team,
in turn surrounded by a circle representing the people they directly supported, and so on, ending with the
outer circle containing the customers
themselves. These circles were con-
nected not only at their center, but
also with a series of radial lines that
indicated cross-functional ties. The

*Peter Drucker has deemed Frances Hesselbein
"...perhaps the best professional manager
in America."*

dynamic looked like a closely woven web, which was prop-
erly symbolic of the values of the organization: The circle is

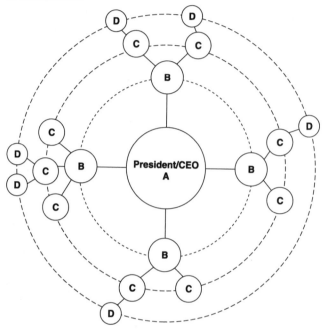

"Circular" Structure Concept
A: President and/or CEO
B: Vice President(s) for Management Unit
     (Management Circle)
C: Group Directors
D: Team Directors

Frances Hesselbein's nonhierarchical organizational design.

inclusive; the circle is tightly woven but flexible, allowing for flow and movement; the circle is organic, as in "family circle," "circle of friends," etc. There is no hierarchy in the circular arrangement, and its spinning nature reflects the spinning of positions within the organization, depending on the specific project under consideration, or other circumstances.[2]

The importance of an organizational design that reflects the unique dynamics of an individual business, while not new, is often underrated. When Nordstrom was preparing to go public in the early seventies, investment bankers were surprised at the lack of a standard organizational chart. As the story goes, the Nordstroms set out to comply with the request, but they quickly realized that it was not representative to arrange the levels and functions in interconnected boxes. They came up with the following illustration of an inverted pyramid and they have stuck with it ever since.

Describing a company as being organized as an upside-down pyramid enjoys today a certain trendiness; however, in 1971 it truly represented the Nordstroms' expectations about how their company would operate. It still graphically reflects the following values of the company:

♦ Recognition of the leading role of the customers.

♦ Importance of _everyone_ in the company supporting the customer.

♦ The closer to the customer, the higher the position.

♦ Notable lack of bureaucratic concerns.

♦ Every management role is a support role.

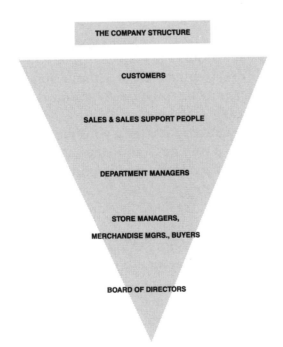

Nordstrom's Inverted Pyramid

Nordstrom's inverted pyramid chart is visible throughout its stores. It hangs in offices and lunchrooms, by time clocks and water coolers. It has appeared in the annual report and in numerous publications. It is a significant paradigm of Nordstrom at its best. More significantly, it provides an invaluable tool at every level. This simple chart conveys the company's culture.

Why not begin the systematic design of service in your organization by engaging your people in describing your potential organizational dynamic? Once the ideal is established, then everybody has a truly effective tool to use as they go about their day-to-day business.

DESIGN THE PEOPLE PROCESSES

Hiring, training, and rewarding are all functions that are traditionally relegated to human resource professionals to design and implement. These parts of your business are vital to your service success and must be integrated fully into the business. People must know what is expected of them before they can set out to achieve it.

The role of the human resource professionals is a supportive role that provides candidates, resources, and follow-through for great ideas. However, the design and execution of the people systems requires the involvement of everybody in management, including you, if the outcome of all the processes is to be service. Human resources is traditionally relegated to a staff function when the responsibilities it includes not only affect the line—they are the line!

Whether your vision is to build spaceships or Space Mountain, to market Chanel or Mickey Mouse, to provide information or entertainment, to heal people's bodies or lighten people's hearts, the key lies in nurturing people to execute the dream. They are out there. In fact, they are undoubtedly already in your employ and, with good

You can dream, create, design and build the most wonderful place in the world...but it requires people to make the dream a reality.
Walt Disney

leadership, will outperform all expectations.

In attempting to systematize the people part of your business, there is a danger of losing the human touch. "Human Resources" has replaced the impersonal-sounding "Personnel" in most companies; yet does the focus on "human" reflect a new sensitivity toward the whole person, or does "resources" indicate a diminution of people to the status of commodities to be managed?

At Nordstrom, the front-line employees are called what they are expected to be—salespeople. Would you rather do business with a clerk or a salesperson? At W.L. Gore & Associates, creators of Gore-Tex, founder Bill Gore encouraged people to designate their own title, and he delightedly supported one hourly employee who called herself the "Supreme Commander of Customer Satisfaction." At Wal★Mart, employees at every level are associates—partners in the business. In addition, the company renamed their human resources function the People Department. There is no confusion at that company about the relative importance of the people to the process.

BUILD THE TEAM

Like all decisions, bringing a new person on board is one that should be made as close to the customer as possible. Hiring should *never* be a staff function. The person responsible for the team should choose the members—plain and simple. No one should be *given* a team member.

If you give people responsibility for the business, you can support their success by letting them build the teams they need. They will know the questions to ask, the experience that is relevant, and the attitudes to probe for. The biggest payoff to the company is that once there is a commitment to hiring a person, there will be a corresponding commitment to that person's success.

There is a well-known incident attributed to Thomas Watson. One of his senior managers made a very large mistake that cost the company millions of dollars in business. The employee nervously began to clear out his desk. When Watson dropped by, the employee couldn't bear more than a couple of minutes of chitchat before he blurted out: "Look, I know why you're here. I'll just offer my resignation and leave." Watson reportedly regarded him with surprising warmth and replied: "You don't really think I would let you go after I just spent three million dollars to train you?!"

TRAIN THE TEAM

Consider your reaction if you were dining in a new restaurant and found a card on the table that said: "Please be patient with us. We are brand new and we're bound to make mistakes, but we will get better." When I found myself in this situation, my first thought was that they had preempted my irritation. However, that charitable reaction was soon replaced with the feeling that they should not have opened unless they were ready to perform flawlessly.

The customer should never be expected to provide the training. Just as it is never acceptable to put someone on the job without the proper preparation, no one should have to plead ignorance to a customer's inquiry. In a previous chapter, the importance of all employees was illustrated by noting the customer interaction with a Disneyland street sweeper. Even though it is generally a short-term position, street sweepers receive several days of training because Disney management knows how many questions they will be asked.

One further thought on training: Make it systematic. Learning opportunities abound. Organize to take advantage of them.

REWARD THE TEAM

The greatest motivator for workers is the knowledge that their performance counts. Two indicators of that are the care with which the working environment is managed and whether or not the necessary tools are provided so that employees are able to do their best work. Beyond that, people must be assured that their behavior has consequences. When employees know that their performance counts, they're more likely to attempt to outperform expectations.

Compensation

If you compare companies with excellent service reputations, you will undoubtedly find as many distinct compensation programs as there are companies. There is no one right way to pay. The keys are consistency, openness, fairness, and the opportunity to share in the growth of the company. People need to be compensated for what they are asked to do, at a rate commensurate with their efforts and their results.

The major element of compensation is pay. To truly provide an incentive, the pay system should reflect the company's philosophy. For example, Nordstrom's philosophy is to give the salespeople the opportunity to be among the highest-paid in their profession nationwide. Entry-level management is paid relatively well, but with less of an edge. The margin of difference disappears as jobs get farther from the customer. Executives are actually paid below market in a system where a salesperson can earn seventy-five thousand dollars a year.

Pay is not the only reward. Other, sometimes more important performance incentives include the following:

- ◆ Promotion opportunities: Good people want an opportunity to grow.
- ◆ Recognition: Take advantage of every possible excuse to celebrate successes.
- ◆ Benefits: Being secure frees people to be successful.
- ◆ Amenities: Workplace atmosphere denotes the level of respect for the individuals working there.
- ◆ Responsibility: Being entrusted to do an important job well is a self-fulfilling prophecy.

If the reward system is designed well, people will be paid what they are worth—and the company will get its money's worth.

ENCOURAGE COMPETITION

If the playing field is level and the rules fair, competition provides the electricity that sets many companies apart.

To be energized, everyone in the company needs to know where it has been, where it is going, and how they can help it get there.

Competition is a dramatic way to clearly define goals and to highlight expectations.

The Nordstroms often laughingly describe their leadership style as "management by contest." It is true that their first reaction to any fresh opportunity, whether it involves naming a department or increasing volume, is to design a competition around it. Nordstrom is a company where there is an amazing depth and breadth of knowledge of goals, and buy-in to achieving them.

Spirited competition can make small achievements worthwhile and seemingly impossible dreams the standard.

As a simple example, on a slow day a five dollar bill could transform the energy level in a Nordstrom's department. The person with the day's first sale would be given the five dollar bill and would be allowed to keep it until someone topped that sale. Suddenly, instead of standing around moaning about how dead business was, lethargic bodies turned into salespeople and customers were attentively served. All for five dollars!

The key is not the size of the prize, but the passion it evokes.

KEEP SCORE

To be energized, everyone in the company needs to know where it has been, where it is going, and how they can help it get there. People need real data in real time. More than anything, management needs to trust them with knowledge.

DESIGN THE WORK ENVIRONMENT

Providing an environment in which employees can focus on serving the customer is often a major step toward improved performance. Do you really want your employees to waste time, energy, and creativity trying to figure out how to get the job done? Do you want customers to have to figure out how to access your business, or worse, to go elsewhere to get what you could have provided?

The work environment should be a pleasant, safe, attractive place for employees and customers alike. Watching traffic patterns, asking questions, and being open to suggestions will help you to maximize the physical plant.

I was proudly showing off our flagship store to a retail executive visiting from Dallas one day. He asked me why we had circulation aisles only around the escalator wells and not leading back into the departments. Struck simultaneously by a strong dose of "But we have always done it this way!" as well as "Nope, not invented here," I gave some kind of nonsensical response. Fortunately, the Store Planning Division was more open, humble, creative, and responsive. Today there are aisles inviting customers to browse in all sections of the stores—and business improved as access improved. Again, even if you are good, how much better can you be if business is designed with improved service in mind?

Everyone is sensitive to their physical environment. Lighting, noise, temperature, cleanliness, and workplace safety condition workers' effectiveness and customers' receptivity. You will save enormous amounts of time and money by inviting customer and employee input on physical plant design in the conceptual stage. If you are already well beyond that, encourage their suggestions for how they would like to improve the present situation.

The complete redo of Nordstrom stores to add abundant holiday decorations means that many regular fixtures have to be pulled off the floor. Every year, John Nordstrom makes the same tour. Every year, he has to collar each store manager and explain why putting all of the excess fixtures in the employees' break rooms simply will not do.

PROVIDE THE TOOLS

People need proper tools to meet your customer care expectations. ServiceMASTER is a company that has achieved legendary service status in fields disdained by most of us: floor mopping, toilet scrubbing, laundry sanitizing, and lawn fertilizing. They have demonstrated superior attention

If 99.9 percent is good enough, then...

♦ **22,000 checks will be deducted from the wrong bank accounts in the next 60 minutes.**

♦ **1,314 phone calls will be misplaced by telecommunication services every minute.**

♦ **12 babies will be given to the wrong parents each day.**

♦ **268,500 defective tires will be shipped this year.**

♦ **20,000 incorrect drug prescriptions will be written in the next 12 months.**[3]

*R*ight from the beginning, I have had a vision of what this business is, and I tell people about it, and I believe in it, and I'm incredibly confident...

Sam Walton

to developing the potential of ordinary workers to provide extraordinary service. One of the keys to ServiceMASTER'S success is their heavy investment in labor-saving equipment for mundane tasks. One example: Workers can clean hospital rooms 20 percent faster than the standard by using Service-MASTER'S pump-activated, soap-dispensing sponge for washing walls and a lighter-weight mop for floors.

The lack of proper tools and equipment was a large part of the problem for the clerks in the White Sale example. Depending on your business, tools can be major items such as adequate computer systems, or they might be something as seemingly insignificant as pens or staples. Employees should be able to reasonably expect the copier to be full of toner and paper, the janitorial service to leave the workplace shining, the coffee to be fresh, and the secretarial assistance to be proficient and professional.

When it comes to providing the optimal equipment, you either pay now or pay later. Think through the process and outfit people up front, or commit to productivity and sales well below potential at escalating costs when work needs to be redone or a "rush" effort is applied to meet a deadline.

The airline industry confounds me in its apparent disregard of available technology. As a very frequent flier, I spend a good part of my travel time standing in lines as each passenger is laboriously processed. And this is when I have confirmed reservations and a preissued boarding card in my possession. To actually have to buy a ticket at the airport is tedious. The agents stand mesmerized before their computer screens, as bit by bit of information is processed and the line grows longer and more anxious.

Contrast this with Southwest Airlines, which for the past several years has been the most (and virtually only) profitable carrier. In addition, Southwest has received the Triple Crown Award for most on time, best baggage handling, and highest passenger rating three years in a row. They have simplified the system to begin with by eliminating seat assignments and by offering self-service touch-screen computers that will allow passengers to book their own flights to most destinations. They are poised to begin ticketless processing. Not constantly beset by anxious, angry passengers whose feet hurt, it is no wonder the Southwest ground crews are such a lot of fun!

PROVIDE THE TECHNOLOGY

The adage in reference to any customer-driven company is "automate the back room and personalize the customer interaction." To distinguish yourself through service today you must have not only the fastest but also the highest-quality systems available to ensure that you can transact your business with your customers with one hundred percent accuracy as expeditiously as possible. At the same time, whether it is a voice on the end of the phone, the message on E-mail, or the surgeon in the operating room, the person connecting with the customer is the key to service delivery. Technology has not yet replaced the person in delivering service. But technology is an invaluable tool the employee must have available.

DESIGN THE MESSAGE

Wherever you find a company that is legendary for its service, you find leadership sharing its passion for the customer at every opportunity. Rather than leaving the dissemination of the service message to chance, leaders personally communicate it at every opportunity. They also pick everyone's brain in their fanatic quest for service perfection. This is true irrespective of industry, personal style, or other circumstances. Nothing lessens

J. Willard Marriott, Sr.

the need for the leader to light the way if service is to be brilliant.

SPREAD THE MESSAGE

J. Willard Marriott, Sr., founder of the namesake hotel chain that institutionalized service theretofore found only in luxury chains, provided a wonderful example. He envisioned quality service and became a spokesperson for it to employees and guests alike. His determination to carry the message to every member of the Marriott staff is legendary—he not only showed up at the front desk during the day, but also appeared in the laundry room at 3:00 a.m. bearing doughnuts and words of appreciation. To stay in touch with guests, he personally reviewed every one of the comment forms and unsolicited letters sent in, and then answered those where a response was appropriate.

Although he may be more reserved than his ebullient father, son J. Willard Marriott, Jr., also recognizes the value of constantly communicating expectations and appreciation, thus he reportedly continues the practices that have set the Marriott chain apart.

TAKE ADVANTAGE OF EVERY OPPORTUNITY

Communicating your passion can take many forms: visiting, coaching, mentoring, modeling, writing, or speaking. It is effective when it is heartfelt, consistent, personal, and direct. It is meant to convey both please—"This is the quality of service we need to achieve"—and thank you—"You are doing great; we couldn't do it without you!"

You may feel shy about your potential to inspire, but inspiration is just what you have to offer. Your people are looking to you for standards, encouragement, enthusiasm, warmth, and appreciation.

SET THE STANDARD

Fabled service leaders recognize that everything the company does communicates the level of its commitment to the customers and to the employees as well. Therefore, they are absolutely uncompromising in their attention to quality.

Take Les Werner, Chairman of the multibillion dollar internationally famous Limited chain. He personally reviews not only every ad, but also scrutinizes every detail of each new store. The dynamic trio of Scott Beck, Jeff Shearer, and Saad Nadhir who in 1993 made Wall Street history when they took their Boston Chicken restaurants public set clear standards for every detail from the secret marinade for their chicken to the polish on the floor.

If fabled companies have a single "secret" weapon, it is this: leadership at all levels that champions quality service at every opportunity.

LISTEN AND LEARN

True communication is always two way: You transmit and you receive. Sometimes people are considered great communicators because of their singular ability to hold us spellbound. However, communication as a leadership tool requires mutuality. You have a great deal of value to share with your people and your customers. Likewise, they have a lot to teach you.

To learn through listening, practice it naively and actively. Naively means that you listen openly, ready to learn something, as opposed to listening defensively, ready to rebut. Listening actively means you acknowledge what you heard and respond accordingly.

EVERYONE IS A MARKETEER

Marketing consists of two basic activities: gathering information and disseminating information. When you maximize the communication opportunities in your company, you turn yourself and your people into a marketing team. Everyone takes responsibility for learning about the customers' preferences and conveying that information throughout the organization. Everyone takes responsibility for conveying what the company is to existing and potential customers.

If fabled companies have a single "secret" weapon, it is this: leadership at all levels that champions quality service at every opportunity. This level of communication occurs through committed and thoughtful exercise of every opportunity to recognize, illustrate, and celebrate doing the right things well.

In the words of Sam Walton, "Communicate everything you can to your associates. The more they know, the more they care. Once they care, there is no stopping them."

REMOVE IMPEDIMENTS, PROVIDE ENHANCEMENTS

Apply this simple test to every part of your operation: Does this process make it easier for your people to do their jobs? Hold everything you are currently doing up to this measure. While everyone knows that a customer focus is critical, this consideration often gets set aside in the rush to implement a major project or to install new equipment. For example, many businesses have devoted enormous resources to Total Quality Management (TQM) in the past few years. One of America's top consultants observed that some of his clients had been working on TQM for over four years without anyone stopping to consider what it would mean for their customers.

If they are to succeed, thoughtfully applied quality principles must evolve from the following:

♦ Attention to process

♦ Commitment to the customer

♦ Involvement of employees

Whether it is TQM or a new employee handbook, reengineering your company or repaving the parking lot, the question must always be asked: Does this make it easier or more difficult for your people to take care of the customer?

Service is often dismissed as the soft side of business. It is often assumed that fabled service companies either are in the right industry for the times or have great spin doctors promoting them. In fact, good service to the customer is not merely hard work, it is hard service as well. It comes from having all systems fine-tuned to the needs of the business. By necessity, it requires continuous improvement and meticulous attention to detail.

Does this make it easier or more difficult for your people to take care of the customer?

Again, let us review what customers expect out of every transaction:

♦ Personal interaction

♦ Operational excellence

♦ Product quality

It is not enough to have well-meaning, very nice people paying attention to the customers' needs. Having the right people is only one part of the equation. Meeting the challenge of providing fabled service means having these excellent people being able to deliver the highest-quality product or service at the very best price. Yes, service is about friendliness and courtesy. But fabled service includes excellent execution and satisfaction.

Remember, service moments of truth cannot be quantified like production quotas or quality standards. They cannot be explicitly managed. Every moment of truth, every contact between your customer and your company is a unique moment. In order to maximize this contact, your people need a thorough grounding in the possible, freedom to make decisions, and practical support.

Do you recall how Nordstrom made this commitment an ever-renewed basis of its culture? Think of their employee handbook: *Rule Number One: Use your own good judgment at all times.*

Finally, the commitment to empowerment is expressed by your ability to get out of the way and allow people to do their jobs. There is an adage about parenting that could well be applied to leading: "What your people need most is roots and wings." The roots come from your firm vision, from being appropriately hired and well trained, from knowing what is expected, from being fully appraised and frequently apprised of where they stand, from being well-compensated for the job they do. This is the foundation of empowerment.

This foundation becomes meaningful only when you allow your people to grow from that point. A key factor common to organizations whose customers marvel at their service is that employees are free to use their own judgment—whether solving a problem, adding value, responding to competition, or personalizing the service. Empowered employees can call upon all of the company's resources to make certain the customer is taken care of—and invited back.

Another way to look at this: Providing your people with firm roots is how you serve them; providing them with wings assures they will serve the customers.

This chapter began by ruminating on where to find good people. Leaders committed to supporting fabled service know that the key is not in the luck of the draw. Good people grow in your organization when you make the commitment to recognize and systematically support the development of that potential. You are committed to giving people roots, then setting them free to succeed in ways that you never dreamed they could.

REFLECTIONS

♦ People's performance from company to company has more to do with the quality of the management than the innate quality of the people themselves.

♦ The front line can't lie: The superstructure reveals the infrastructure.

♦ To thrill to the care of your customers means to have what they want when they want it.

♦ Design service into the system from the start.

♦ The hallmarks of systems that support service are simplicity and relevance.

♦ Service becomes systemic when designed into the organization's structure, processes, goals and expectations, and work environment.

ACTION STEPS

Redesign your organizational structure to reflect your commitment to the customer. Involve all constituents in the process.

Collaborate on the vision and mission of the company. Strategies and goals should be consistent with the reason you are in business.

Test strategies, products, and processes against customer perceptions before implementing.

Always ask: "How can we do this better?" Then listen to the answers.

Establish an ongoing forum for your employees to communicate what works and what does not.

Eradicate red tape—with a vengeance!

Commitment:
To Be in Business to Serve Society

♦ Demonstrate personal integrity
♦ Act in accordance with your principles
♦ Serve society

FABLED SERVICE IS INSEPARABLE FROM INTEGRITY

---

*To give real service, you must add something which
cannot be bought or measured with money,
and that is sincerity and integrity.*

Donald A. Adams

6

THE ISSUE

Quality service can only be realized in an organizational culture that values integrity. Serving customers well only truly happens when an organization sincerely believes that this is how customers deserve to be served. If service is used as a come-on or merely as a competitive advantage, it will never be the core of the business.

The company must exhibit a win-win attitude. If it is good for the customer, it is good for the company, and vice versa. It is obvious to all stakeholders whether or not the company is sincerely pursuing the best interests of the customers or merely looking for a quick buck.

Some sensitive areas regarding integrity are pricing, advertising, and bait-and-switch tactics. More intrinsic to the company's self-concept are the company's philosophy and

Business Leaders 1890-1990

Charles E. Merrill	Merrill Lynch
Elizabeth Arden	Elizabeth Arden
A.P. Giannini	Bank of America
Frank McNamera	Diners Club
Ray Kroc	McDonald's
Joyce C. Hall	Hallmark
Edward L. Bunoys	Public Relations
John D. Rockefeller, Jr.	Philanthropist
Alfred P. Sloan, Jr.	General Motors
Louis B. Mayer	MGM
Henry Luce	Time, Inc.
William Paley	CBS
Robert DeGraff	Simon & Schuster
Thomas J. Watson, Sr.	IBM
Henry Ford	Ford

policies toward employees, which must be formulated carefully and reexamined frequently. Companies that operate with integrity are focused on the underlying principle of fairness for all constituencies, at all times.

THE IMPACT OF BUSINESS

In 1990, *Life* published a special edition honoring the one hundred most influential people of our century. In this age of astounding technology, industry, and commerce, very few businesspeople made the list. This lack of business and industry leadership is striking given the enormous influence business has over people, processes, products, and capital.

Consider the following:

♦ Some businesses produce annual revenues well in excess of the GNP of smaller industrialized nations.

♦ Wal★Mart's associate base of close to one half-million rivals the population of five American states.

♦ Legend has it that McDonald's considered adding fried onion rings to its menu but scrapped the idea because their volume of business would have depleted the entire worldwide supply of onions.

Even in a small business, a manager's domain is significant. For example, the management of a fast-food outlet might require the employment of thirty people and the use of thousands of pounds of raw food to produce over one million dollars in sales annually. Running a department in a successful store might require the management of fifty people who sell fifteen million dollars of merchandise annually. A single property manager might be responsible for several million dollars of real estate.

Perhaps it is unrealistic for most of us to aspire to join the ranks of the one hundred most influential people in this century, but each of us can demonstrate integrity by using our power and influence within our communities for the greater good.

The news is filled with examples of great moral, political, and social leaders. One of the most well-known paragons of servant leadership in the world today is Mother Teresa. Like legends of every magnitude, she is powerful because of her focus on service.

The key to enduring, effective use of power seems to be personal integrity. If your commitment to service leadership is to make a significant difference in your life and the lives of others, you must demonstrate personal integrity.

AP/Wide World Photos

Mother Teresa feeds a bottle to a baby at a shelter for abandoned and abused children in New York City.

WHAT DO WE MEAN BY INTEGRITY?

Winston Churchill demonstrated the depth of his integrity by never losing sight of his customers, namely his countrymen. We might glean a significant insight from his own words:

> *The key to your impact as a leader is your own sincerity.*
> *Before you can inspire with emotion, you*
> *must be swamped with it yourself.*
> *Before you can move their tears, your own must flow.*
> *To convince them, you must yourself believe.*

INTEGRITY IS AUTHENTICITY

Many managers lack personal conviction about the value of the principles they want their people to adopt. Rather than belabor this unfortunate and common attitude, consider instead the far too rare examples of leaders whose commitment to service is part of their essence.

- ♦ ITEM: You commit to the equal opportunity for both men and women to advance in your company. However, all of the crucial meetings are automatically scheduled at 7 a.m., when a 7:30 a.m. starting time would allow those with children to arrange childcare.
- ♦ ITEM: The company's mission statement says that the customer comes first, yet all of the prime parking places are reserved for senior management.
- ♦ ITEM: You make impassioned speeches to your employees about their importance, but you do not know them by name, not even the old-timers.
- ♦ ITEM: A medical supply company facing bankruptcy makes a last-ditch effort to turn its business around by planning a company-wide meeting on service and teamwork. The autocratic and remote executives are surprised when it is suggested that scheduling an all-day meeting the last Saturday before Christmas might not be the motivational turnaround they seek. Instead of changing the date, they post a notice that meeting attendance is mandatory and the penalty for noncompliance is termination. They, of course, are not in attendance—they already know all about service and teamwork.

To Churchill's moving words, a service leader might want to add: Before you can ask others to serve with joy, you must dedicate yourself to their service. Before you can inspire others to love your customers, you must demonstrate your passion.

Integrity can mean many things: being consistent, taking an ethical approach to your business, performing as promised, or just being whole and sound.

INTEGRITY IS CONSISTENCY

First consider the challenge to be consistent: to practice what you profess. Service integrity is demonstrated by how you handle the small things, as well as the large.

Here is a personal example of how this dynamic works. The Nordstroms have always stressed the importance of family. When the Nordstroms offered me the opportunity to open the California market, they expressed their values very clearly. Although this was arguably the most exciting challenge in the company to date, they presented it almost apologetically: "Your family is so important to you and provide you such strength. If this move is difficult for them to make, please turn down this opportunity. We understand, and we'll work out a better move for you."

Their concern for me as a whole person made an enormous impression on me. In the ensuing years when I asked thousands of people to relocate for the company, I could ensure that these moves worked well for them and their families knowing that I had the Nordstroms' full support.

INTEGRITY IS ETHICS

One characteristic that distinguishes service leaders is their simple honesty. Often, their adherence to basic principles of decency and honesty is so out of step with existing norms that their behavior appears quaint. When tough bosses are acclaimed for their fanatical pursuit of profit, regardless of the price, it is helpful to remember that long-term success seems to belong to those who do not take ethical shortcuts.

WHAT PRICE INTEGRITY?

"Everybody does it!" is the oft-heard excuse for moral malfeasance. Yet everybody certainly is not doing it, or doing the wrong thing would not be news.

Time after time, we are shocked to find our heroes featured on the newspaper's front

DRABBLE® by Kevin Fagan
DRABBLE reprinted by permission of UFS, Inc.

© 1992 United Feature Syndicate, Inc.

page or on television's evening news because they have taken liberties with the law in their pursuit of happiness and success. At that point, no matter how impressive their prior achievements, they have compromised their ability to lead.

It is easy to rationalize unethical behavior with the belief that the end justifies the means. This slippery slope is so pervasive that an ethics professor in graduate school let our class in on the secret: Business ethics is an oxymoron; according to him, the ultimate test against which you should weigh decisions and actions is "Can I do this and keep my job?"

Ethical leadership supports another standard: Can you do this and keep your integrity intact? The expectation of everyone at every level is that they should be their best. Doing well by doing good becomes the challenge.

Every business has "gray areas" where laws or policies are one thing but the encouraged practice is another:

- ♦ Promising delivery dates to secure an order, whether or not they are achievable
- ♦ Advertising money-back guarantees, but reprimanding employees who honor them
- ♦ Devising phony price comparisons or pricing products or services as high as the market will bear
- ♦ Training salespeople to make false or misleading presentations
- ♦ Tolerating expense padding
- ♦ Sharing copyrighted software or otherwise misappropriating supplies or equipment

Some of these practices are management directives. Some come about because no one is paying attention. No matter the genesis, the results are the same: Compromising ethical standards fatally weakens a company's morale. Employees learn that if they cannot trust their managers' basic honesty, they cannot trust them in anything. That cynicism is inevitably transferred to the customers and offsets all the money poured into customer relations efforts.

LACK OF INTEGRITY IS DISINTEGRATION

Acting with integrity is not a theoretical pursuit. Rather than intellectualizing or rationalizing actions, simply pay attention to your guts. If you are not acting with integrity, there is usually an instinctual physical response.

The symptoms of stress are often described as "falling apart" or "coming apart at the seams." Perhaps you become anxious, edgy, nervous, or display other symptoms of stress. You feel off balance, as if you are running as fast as you can and getting nowhere. Medical studies corroborate that during times of high stress and low function, people are far more likely to become seriously ill. Sickness, in turn, puts additional stress on the situation, which then deteriorates further.

When a company operates against its principles, the same lack of focus and efficiency can be observed. Corporate symptoms of malaise could include

- ◆ Excessive bureaucracy
- ◆ Focus on command and control versus partnership
- ◆ Endless politicking
- ◆ Red tape
- ◆ Low morale
- ◆ Low productivity

INTEGRATION IS FOCUS

People who act in accordance with their principles and who are engaged in an activity that they love are centered and strong. Being secure in what you do attracts others to want to be part of your efforts. An internal gyroscope alerts you when you are getting off center and aids you in steering a straight course toward your goals.

If you are focused, your company also develops strong characteristics, such as the following.

The core idea of fairness. A conviction that everyone deserves a fair shake at all times is a commitment to service both within the company and without. If fairness is the accepted standard, people can focus on what's the best for everyone.

A commitment to the win-win dynamic. Thinking "If you win, I lose" is a big impediment to maximizing service potential. If something is good for the customer, it has to be good for the company. Whether you are talking about power, compensation, customers, products, or success, if it can be shared, it will increase.

High productivity. When you love what you do, you find the energy to do it well. When you lead others in something you love, you transmit that energy to them, and they in turn do it well.

High quality. If you have your heart in something, you have the highest standard for it. Be it your child or your brainchild, if it comes from you, you want it to be the best.

High standards. If you pursue integrity in all that you do, not only will you have the highest expectations of your own performance, but also of the performance of others. The entire effort and outcome will be compromised if you allow any part of the team to slack off. The question always arises: In a people-centered environment, can you be tough enough? The answer is, you can't be too tough.

Lots of fun. By definition, can you have passion without enthusiasm? Enthusiasm means literally "imbued with spirit." Enthusiasm imbues well integrated businesses with a spirit of celebration. It may be dignified or it may be raucous; it depends on the intrinsic nature of the business. One thing we know, it won't be dull.

Consistency without conformity. Adherence to a strong, central set of core principles assures a consistent standard of quality throughout the organization. Everyone knows what is expected, and therefore they can come to rely on the company. This consistency is also freeing. Because the core is so strong, the superficial details are left to the individual. This promotes ownership and creativity.

REFLECTIONS

♦ Experience and history show that you can lead service excellence only if you value integrity.

♦ Consider these words from two cultures vastly separated by time, geography, and technology:

> *Wealth does not bring goodness, but goodness*
> *wealth and every other blessing,*
> *both to the individual and the state.*

Socrates, 469-399 B.C.

> *We are not in business to make maximum*
> *profit for our shareholders. We are in business*
> *for only one reason—to serve society.*
> *If business does not serve society,*
> *society will not long tolerate our profits,*
> *not even our existence.*

Kenneth Dayton, restating Socrates, A.D. 1975

ACTION STEPS

Where there is dissonance between your company's principles and your personal principles, align with the higher value.

Communicate your standards clearly, both in word and deed.

Insist on adherence to standards; it is imperative for success at your company.

Trust your instincts. You will feel balanced when you operate with integrity.

Have your heart in your work and your work in your heart.

Commitment:
To Create and Sustain the Vision

♦ The importance of vision
♦ What makes a leader?
♦ Leadership in action
♦ The leader as server

FABLED SERVICE IS EMPOWERED BY LEADERSHIP

The first responsibility of a leader is to define reality.
The last is to say thank you. In between the two,
the leader must become a servant and a debtor.
That sums up the progress of an artful leader.

Max De Pree

7

THE ISSUE

We have come full circle. We began by exploring the commitment to make service our way of life and we end by committing to lead service. In between, we have examined steps that demonstrate our commitment to be of service. With each step, we develop our ability to be service leaders.

The helix that always brings you back around past the place where you began, yet always further ahead on the path, is the dynamic of leading continuous improvement, of running the learning organization, of searching to be ever more excellent at the helm. It is the path of both personal and corporate growth. What is it that you now know about being a fabled service leader, at the end of your journey?

♦ Demonstrate what you want others to become.

- Service is defined by your customers.

- Look outside of your customer base and industry for ways to improve your service.

- Manage all of your resources with a focus on service.

- Your commitment to serve and the way you live out that commitment must be authentic.

- To lead service requires a continual and decisive recommitment.

TRADITIONAL OR TRANSFORMATIONAL LEADER?

There are numerous models of fabled service leaders across all businesses and industries. They built their businesses by finding something they really enjoyed doing and could do well. They engaged others in the same pursuit. Customers responded positively and gave them impetus to continue to stretch their vision. They stayed focused on the game, ignoring all the cheers from the stands and the media accolades.

We shall not cease from exploration
And the end of all our exploring
Will be to arrive at where we started
And to know the place for the first time.[1]

Yet, these modest, largely intuitive people built their businesses in a way that is considered revolutionary today. Think of Bill Gore of W.L. Gore & Associates, who was delighted when members of his flat organization designated their own titles and came up with such whoppers as "Supreme Commander." Consider the incredibly productive creativity at such places as 3M in the early days under former Chairman of the Board Bill McKnight or the overwhelming effectiveness of the turned-on team at IBM, inspired by their visionary founder, Thomas Watson, Sr.

The very structures, values, and outcomes that are being called revolutionary today have been the basis for fabled service throughout history: These are the organizations that

have mastered how to work with their people to create the customer-serving vision.
These are the companies that dedicate themselves to sustaining that vision and nurturing it through the hand-off to successive
generations.

The most important lesson is to attend to the basics of customer-driven, vision-fueled leadership.

ESSENTIAL ELEMENTS OF LEADERSHIP

The companies used as examples throughout this book have
practiced the simple, essential business processes so effectively that what has become traditional for them has created
a revolution for those of us who have gotten away from the
basics. Quite simply, businesses that dedicate themselves to
serving the customers best—and succeed at doing so—not
only survive, but provide vivid lessons for us all. The most
important lesson is to attend to the basics of customer-driven,
vision-fueled leadership.

In his book, _Certain Trumpets: The Call of Leaders,_ Garry
Wills's thesis of his study of leadership is as follows: "The
leader is one who mobilizes others toward a goal shared by
leaders and followers....Leaders, followers and goals make
up the three equally necessary supports for leadership."[2]

> Leaders... Followers... Goals.
> Visionary leaders... Engaged followers... Shared goals.
> Leaders who mobilize others toward shared goals...
> Followers who are capable of responding...
> Goals that are worthwhile sharing and striving for.

Garry Wills calls these elements the three legs of the leadership stool—remove one, and you don't have leadership. You
might have management. Or dictatorship, or anarchy. Leadership only occurs when the three legs balance.

TODAY'S HEROIC LEADER

No temperament, educational or ethnic background, gender or age predisposes a person to lead a fabled service organization. However, there is one distinguishing characteristic. The urge to serve others is the defining element of service leadership. It also seems to be the element that, in the end, discourages so many would-be aspirants. It is on this rock that the professed desire to run a fabled service organization breaks into mere lip service. The path to service leadership then becomes twisted, the footsteps indistinct or even misleading, and the destination obscure.

True heroism is remarkably sober, very undramatic. It is not the urge to surpass all others at whatever cost, but the urge to serve others at whatever cost.[3]

In a *Fortune* magazine cover story dedicated to what he calls "the new post-heroic leadership," writer John Huey gives a startling statistic: "Ninety-five percent of American managers today say the right thing. Five percent do it."[4]

What is this "right thing" that virtually all managers talk about, but a mere five percent actually do? The "right thing" probably has not changed over the years, but the importance of doing it has increased exponentially.

Traditional Leaders (95%)	Fabled Service Leaders (5%)
Focus on power	Focus on empowerment
Top of the hierarchy	Center of the circle
Autocratic	Participative
Exclusive	Inclusive
Seek deference	Seek consensus
Conscious of rights	Conscious of responsibility
Inwardly focused	Other focused
Bureaucratic	Entrepreneurial

To sum up prevailing wisdom, a leader's job is to

♦ Envision and articulate just what the company is trying to accomplish, and

♦ Create the environment in which employees can share responsibility and the rewards of doing it well.

This evolving leadership style takes many names: transformational leadership, participative leadership, servant leadership, or post-heroic or even virtual leadership. Post-heroic is an important term for us to consider. It sounds strange to consider the hero as being obsolete when you are focusing on the leadership of fabled service. Yet any legendary service leader would profess that you need to look beyond the leader as the lone hero, to find a heroic vision and the heroes among the people who share the responsibility and the glory for realizing that vision.

> [Post-heroic leadership] still requires many of the attributes that have always distinguished the best leaders—intelligence, commitment, energy, courage of conviction, integrity—but here's the big difference: It expects those qualities of just about everybody in the organization.[5]

TODAY'S LEADER AND POWER

If everyone in the organization is expected to demonstrate leadership qualities, where does the person in charge derive the power to get the job done?

Effective leaders are not concerned about the locus of power. In healthy companies, there is little concern for titles, perquisites, office trappings, number of direct reports, or any of the other external signs that one person is important and another is not. Effective leaders' focus is on what is critical to the mission: A person's real ability and use of that ability to encourage others to contribute their best to the effort. This power resides in the person, not in the position. This power grows, not because it is hoarded, but

Five Sources of Power [6]

Derived from the position you hold:

♦ **Power to reward**
♦ **Power to punish**
♦ **Power that is authority, i.e., "Because I said so!" power**

Inherent in the person you are:

♦ **Power deriving from expertise**
♦ **Referent power that comes from being a positive role model**

because it is shared. The power base is broad, stable, and relevant to the mission at hand.

THE LEADER AS STEWARD

The paradigm of the steward is the most helpful model to follow as you commit to living out these values. Peter Block defines stewardship as "...a way to use power to serve through the practice of partnership and empowerment."[7] Stewardship also implies acceptance of the responsibility for certain assets, with the expectation that at the end of your watch, you will hand them on in more abundance and in better condition than you received them. When you think of yourself as a steward, you do not expect honor to accrue to you because you have taken the responsibility. Rather, you feel honored to be involved in something so worthy of your time and talents.

We have considered partnership and empowerment on each step of this quest for service leadership. Applying these concepts to the definition of stewardship means accepting accountability for results without resorting to controlling or caretaking behavior.

THE ASSETS

What assets are at your disposal?

Physical plant	Finances
Product	Vision
Reputation	Future environment
Franchise	Information

It is fortunate that the enormity of this responsibility is shared and that those who are co-responsible with us are empowered and energized to succeed.

How Do You Lead the Customer-Driven Organization?

The key is not what you know, but that you commit to act on your knowledge and beliefs. In the words of John Huey: "Leadership involves getting things started and facilitating change."[8] Leadership is about putting the right things into practice and developing momentum toward a shared, meaningful goal. You lead by doing a few very powerful things, over and over again, perfecting them with practice.

Envisioning

Everthing begins in the mind of the practical dreamer, the possibility thinker. Jack Welch, the legendary leader of General Electric, minces no words on the subject:

> *Great leaders create a vision; articulate*
> *that vision; passionately own that vision;*
> *and relentlessly drive it to completion.*

Great leaders also share their visions in such a way that they can be enlarged and owned by everyone involved. Remember where true power lies. In order to inspire people to follow, you must champion a worthwhile vision that improves the lot of all those who share in it.

Acting

Bill Gore says it clearly: "Leadership's a verb, not a noun." Tom Peters uses the phrase "bias for action" to describe one of the key characteristics of successful companies. Leaders are quite clearly people who make certain things get done.

Grade your actions based on what they actually contribute to revenues. This can prevent you from demanding things that contribute nothing to the business at hand. Bureaucracy is the wet blanket on the flame of vision fanned into action! Your mission should be to stomp out bureaucracy, not originate it.

Expecting

Two businesses with the same employment pool consistently have different results. The disappointed one laments over the poor caliber of "help" available. The successful one shares its vision and inspires people with the valuable contribution required to achieve that vision. If you expect the best from everyone, you will release more ability and energy than you can ever exhaust.

Get a good idea, and stay with it. Dog it, and work at it until it's done and done right.

Walt Disney

Deciding

When all the opinions have been voiced and the issues aired, the leader weighs all factors and makes the decision that is the most responsive to the stewardship of all the assets. Consensus building is the beginning of the responsibility; deciding what to do is the outcome.

The more decentralized the decision making, the more critical the strong central direction. The closer to the customer the decision making gets, the more decisive a leader must be. The leader has to clearly articulate the direction, standards, and overarching commitment of the company. Employees are free to make good immediate decisions when boundaries are clearly defined and understood. Companies who lead in customer care possess clear values and systems designed and fine-tuned to support that clarity.

Sustaining the Vision

The key to sustaining the vision is sharing it, from its creation through its implementation to its regeneration. The vision must be shared on an ongoing basis with all those who are involved. In the long-term, a sense of shared vision should be the primary focus when the responsibility for leadership is passed on.

LEADERS MAKE A LIFETIME COMMITMENT

You cannot borrow an appropriate service vision. You must participate in the development of a unique vision for the company you lead. You must commit yourself to breathing life into that vision. You must express that vision throughout every part of your business. Nobody—not customer, employee, shareholder, or casual observer—should question what drives you. You must pursue that vision to completion and begin the process again.

Of course, there is no compulsion to do any of this except for the recurring realization that the potential for fabled service is not being realized. What stands in the way of dedicating your energies and time to providing a very different kind of place to work and to transact business? Why not enter into a meaningful partnership with employees, a partnership that recognizes what great things you all can bring to bear? Suppose you extended this partnership to your customers, making satisfying their needs the fulfillment of everyone's dreams. If you did all this, how would it affect your life? The lives of your children? The next generations'?

You can take the familiar path, well worn and beckoning. Or you can strike out where the way is much fainter but the destination appears far more significant. The footprints you are leaving are a real encouragement to those who follow.

While stewardship is a challenging model, the opportunity to develop available resources to their fullest is a worthy effort. In pursuing these commitments to leading fabled service, you will be calling on the best in yourself and in others.

> *In the final resolve, enjoy true success in your life: the success that comes through supporting the success of others.*

REFLECTIONS

♦ Fabled service leaders master how to work with their people to create the customer-serving vision.

♦ The urge to serve others is the defining element of service leadership.

♦ The key to fabled service leadership is making the commitment to act on your knowledge and beliefs.

ACTION STEPS

Work with people to set and achieve high goals and exceed personal expectations.

Delegate authority and responsibility.

Clear hurdles to success.

Encourage risk taking.

Provide all tools necessary for success.

Motivate through inspiring vision.

See the best in and expect the best from everyone.

Recognize accomplishments; show appreciation.

Epilogue

Several years ago I read an editorial in *The Wall Street Journal* that in a few paragraphs captured what I recognized as the underlying imperatives of fabled service. The author challenged me to remember three things always:

- ♦ I am the customer.

- ♦ I am the company.

- ♦ My goal needs to be to create service that is not just the best, but legendary.[1]

I carried that clipping around until it disintegrated. These emphatic thoughts became the basis for my remarks whenever I shared thoughts on service with any audience. I would like to close my reflections on leading fabled service by making these three challenges the final call to action.

These three points call to everybody at every level. This is a blueprint for service leadership that will call forth the capability of everyone in the company. There is no "they" in an organization dedicated to fabled service. If you are the customer, you recognize, respect, and welcome your customers' expectations. If you are the company, you rejoice in the challenge to respond to your customers, with confidence in the abundant resources at your disposal to do so more effectively than anyone else. If you are committed to providing service that goes beyond good and even beyond the best, you are open to the endless possibilities to grow and improve.

The single largest impediment to providing sustained fabled service is success. When you become successful, when your customers begin to delight in topping each other's stories about their experiences with you, when your people are told over and over that they are the best, when you are lionized by the media—you begin to lose touch with reality. You grow beyond the customer. You redefine the company. You become satisfied that you have reached fabled status, even though by definition, "The point about 'legendary' (service) is that it presents a goal that is always moving ahead and never will be attained...Legendary gives everyone who deals with customers a rich sense of the possibilities."[2]

Leading your company to the level of fabled service should be a worthwhile goal for everyone. Every day people are taking care of people as they go about their ordinary course of business. With attention to responding specifically to their customers' needs, with warmth and humor, with perspective and gratitude, these people perform ordinary acts that produce extraordinary outcomes. Productivity is heightened. Well-being is improved. Knowledge is shared. Anxiety is lessened. These individual and corporate acts of kindness, professionalism, effort, and encouragement raise the bar at the same time that they reward all who participate in them. They provide service that customers talk about— and thus pass on into fables that will in turn sustain and nourish yet new levels of people making the customer the reason for their business.

Notes

CHAPTER 1

1. R. Keith Denton and Charles Boyd, *Did You Know? Fascinating Facts and Fallacies About Business*, Prentice-Hall, Englewood Cliffs, New Jersey, 1994.

2. Ibid.

3. Burt Nanus, *Visionary Leadership*

CHAPTER 2

1. Tom Peters, "On Excellence, Achieving Excellence in an Instant," *The Seattle Times* (November 15, 1993).

2. Sam Walton from *Made in America* as quoted in *Fortune* (June 29, 1992).

CHAPTER 3

1. Peter Gumbel and Richard Turner, "Blundering Mouse," *The Wall Street Journal* (March 10, 1994).

2. Technical Assistance Research Programs, quoted in Karl Albrecht and Ron Zemke, *Service America!* Dow Jones-Irwin, Homewood, Illinois, 1985. Reprinted with permission.

3. Michael Treacy and Fred Wiersma, "Customer Intimacy and Other Value Disciplines," *Harvard Business Review* (January-February 1993).

4. Reprinted with permission from THE PRYOR REPORT, Vol. 10, No. 4a.

5. Sam Walton, Wal★Mart Associate Handbook, 1994.

6. Stanley Marcus, "Buyers Should Be Sellers."

CHAPTER 4

1. Max De Pree as quoted in William Safire and Leonard Safire, *Leadership*, Simon & Schuster, New York, 1990.

2. Theodore Hesburgh, president, Notre Dame

3. Sam Walton

4. Peter Drucker as quoted in William Safire and Leonard Safire, *Leadership*, Simon & Schuster, New York, 1990.

5. From a speech by Tom Peters at Santa Clara University, 1986.

6. Nordstrom Employee Handbook

7. Sam Walton

8. 1990 Nordstrom, Inc. Annual Report, pp. 4, 6, 10, 11.

CHAPTER 5

1. Sam Walton

2. Frances Hesselbein, CEO Girl Scouts of America

3. *Insight,* Syncrude Canada Ltd., Communications Division. Reprinted with permission.

CHAPTER 7

1. T.S. Eliot from "Little Gidding" in *The Complete Poems and Plays*, Harcourt Brace Jovanovich, New York, 1980.

2. Garry Wills, *Certain Trumpets: The Call of Leaders*, Simon & Schuster, New York, 1994.

3. Reader's Digest, August 1994.

4. John Huey, "The New Post-Heroic Leadership," *Fortune* (February 21, 1994).

5. Ibid.

6. Thomas A. Stewart, "New Ways to Exercise Power," *Fortune* (November 6, 1989). ©1989 Time Inc. All rights reserved.

7. Peter Block, *Stewardship*, Berrett-Koehler Publishers, San Francisco, California, 1993.

8. John Huey, op cit.

EPILOGUE

1. Paul Hawkens, in a *The Wall Street Journal* article about one of his books.

2. Ibid.

Index